A WAY
FORWARD

ANNA VOIGT is an internationally published author and poet with a passion for the mysticism of Nature, the sacred Feminine, and the connection between creative expression, healing and spirituality. Anna has had extensive training and practice in the creative and healing arts and follows the path of Self-enquiry. She holds graduate degrees in Arts and Communications and among her publications are **Wisdom From The Earth**, **New Visions New Perspectives**, **Fire and Shadow**, and **Simple Meditation**.

NEVILL DRURY is especially interested in visionary consciousness and the mystical wisdom traditions. A former editor of **Nature & Health** magazine, he holds a Masters degree from Macquarie University, Sydney, and his work has been translated into many different languages. His most recent books include **Exploring the Labyrinth**, **Creating Good Karma**, **Reincarnation**, **Creative Visualization**, and **The Shaman's Quest**.

A WAY FORWARD

Spiritual Guidance for
Our Troubled Times

Anna Voigt and Nevill Drury

Red Wheel
Boston, MA / York Beach, ME

CONTENTS

INTRODUCTION

With the rise of international terrorism, the unstable nature of world politics and the critical state of our global environment, it is clear that we live in increasingly dangerous times. The world is becoming more polarized, and it is also true that we now possess greater capacities for self-destruction than we have ever possessed before. The world is a deeply troubled place and many people feel increasingly insecure, fearful and disempowered. This can contribute to a sense of struggle and confusion, as we search for ways of finding purpose, meaning and peace in our lives. If ever there was a time for spiritual reflection, contemplation and positive action, that time is *now*.

Media reports remind us daily of the ongoing international conflicts relating to disputed territories and resources, and the animosity and aggression expressed towards minorities and those who embrace different religious beliefs. These personal and social problems have surfaced again and again in different parts of the world, through all periods of history. Such conflicts cause immeasurable pain, grief and suffering. As well as these continuing global conflicts and uncertainties, the inevitable losses that we all experience as part of life add to our confusion and despair.

However, on another level of human understanding, many of us are beginning to realize that our wars and battles are also conflicts within ourselves. And until we can learn to transform ourselves, and search for the deepest wisdom that is available to us – the profound and authentic lessons of the Spirit – how can there truly be hope for the world at large?

Traditionally, the established religions have provided a framework for spiritual expression, guidance and support. However, in recent times, some of these religious ideologies and practices have come increasingly into question. Also, spirituality can embrace a wide range of thoughts, feelings and experiences – from deeply felt encounters with Nature to the directly mystical – whereas following a traditional religion can sometimes be restrictive. Wisdom can come to us from many directions, from ancient sources to contemporary insights, so spirituality is essentially about being open to the diverse aspects of existence, about learning from direct experience and being guided from within, and ultimately about awakening to one's innately divine nature.

Whatever path we take, it is clear we will have to change our priorities in responding to the critical problems that now exist across the globe – problems created by the ways human beings are currently living. As Anne Bancroft has written, "We need to work at self-transformation while at the same time we must put right injustices in the world, feed the starving, and restore the forests. The inner and the outer must begin to act in harmony together."

For many centuries we have existed in a severely unbalanced world where masculine thinking and values have dominated to the exclusion and devaluing of feminine values. According to the ancient wisdom traditions, all human beings have a masculine energetic principle and a feminine energetic principle.

This natural inner dynamic is expressed in different ways in different cultures. For example, in Chinese philosophy this understanding is expressed in the *I Ching*, and through the well-known symbol of the Tao, which incorporates the energies of *Yin* – feminine, and *Yang* – masculine. In the West, a similar understanding is expressed in Jungian psychology where the individual psyches of both men and women have their feminine and masculine aspects – known as the *anima* and *animus* respectively. Broadly speaking, the feminine aspects are concerned with *being* and the masculine aspects with *doing* ...

As Laurence Boldt has explained, "In the Jungian conception, the masculine aspect of self is concerned with *controlling* the external world. Technology is the pre-eminent means of achieving control. In a society where masculine values dominate, technology is highly valued and advanced. The feminine aspect of self is concerned with enlarging the individual's *experience* of the world as it is – that is, with being. In a society where masculine values dominate, people have little experience with being ..."

According to Carl Jung the key to attaining psychological maturity is to achieve a state of balance between male and female energies. It is vital for men to discover their inner feminine qualities and for women to explore their masculine dynamics. While there has been some changes in recent times in re-assessing traditional female and male roles, to date there has been little change in the structure of our major social and political institutions, so that women are still struggling to operate within frameworks that are predominantly masculine in their definitions. Clearly, our religious, corporate and political institutions require a complete overhaul in order to reflect feminine values as well as masculine values. The challenge now is to bring a more inclusive, holistic and nurturing approach into an apparently hostile world and to allow renewed feelings of interrelationship, interconnectedness and a reverence for the planet to pervade our lives.

Many of us sense that the world is undergoing a major transition and we feel caught up in a type of limbo between the crumbling of the old world order and the birthing of the new. In ancient China, the crucial time between cultures – the ending of one civilization and the beginning of another – was known as Wei Chi. As Soozi Holbeche has commented, "Wei Chi was considered to be the midpoint between life and death and was therefore a time of crisis and danger. However, Wei Chi was also regarded as a major initiation, a time for choice and an opportunity for change." This is also of great relevance to the world today, for one of the most important choices we have to make now is between clinging to the apparent, but illusory, safety of the past, or taking the risk of leaping forward into the unknown, and conducting our lives in a new and more harmonious way.

Writer Susan Jeffers suggests that there are three important realities to embrace in dealing with uncertainty, and without an understanding of these realities, it is very difficult, if not impossible, to make yourself comfortable with all the uncertainty in the world. Jeffers describes these three realities: "that the only certainty is that life is uncertain – there are no guarantees; that once you surrender to the fact that you are unable to control the uncertainty, you will, at last, be able to breathe a sigh of relief; and a deep acceptance that life is uncertain opens the door to a powerful way of living."

We face the challenge now to adopt new levels of truth, integrity and compassion, to move beyond judging those whom we perceive to be different as inferior or evil, and to accept and celebrate the diversity of life and culture on this beautiful planet. We are also called now to move beyond the limitations of our old belief systems – beliefs which have constricted the way in which we relate to the world – and to adopt values which embrace change, openness, flexibility and love.

> All the heavens and all the
> hells are within you.
>
> JOSEPH CAMPBELL

Always say "yes" to the present moment.
What could be more futile, more insane, than to create
inner resistance to something that already is?
What could be more insane than to oppose life itself,
which is now and always now? Surrender to what is.
Say "yes" to life – and see how life suddenly starts
working for you rather than against you. Whatever the
present moment contains, accept it as if you had
chosen it. Always work with it, not against it.
Make it your friend and ally, not your enemy.
This will miraculously transform your whole life.

ECKHART TOLLE

THE QUEST
FOR PERSONAL MEANING
AND PURPOSE

We each discover meaning and purpose in our own way.
However, because we live in an increasingly global society
where we are discovering the interconnectedness and interrelationship between all things – rather than the usual view of seeing the
world as if we are independent and separate individuals – there are
issues and processes that affect us all and from which we can all
learn. So it is surely worth considering those perspectives that have
the potential to provide our lives with a greater sense of depth,
integrity and personal authenticity.

Most of us are very effectively socialized by prevailing cultural
norms. We learn early on that our survival in everyday life depends
primarily upon establishing our persona – a specific, socially

acceptable version of ourselves that we present to the world. We also learn to promote this personal image of ourselves in order to achieve our personal goals. In doing this, particularly in more competitive societies, many of us become increasingly driven, and often more aggressive, as we seek to get further ahead in our quest for personal advancement.

Nevertheless, despite any material gains we may achieve through this competitive process, sooner or later we need to ask ourselves whether our life has a true meaning or purpose. Sooner or later we are going to have to ask ourselves *who we really are and what we are doing with our lives.*

Do we define ourselves mostly in terms of our material prosperity, our possessions, the acquisition of specific skills or our level of seniority in the workplace? Or are we more inclined to consider the quality of our relationships and the impact our thoughts and actions may have on our family, friends and the wider community – and perhaps even on future generations – and to explore where we fit in within the broader scheme of things?

Every being is created
for a purpose, and the light
of that purpose is already kindled
in this soul.

SA'ADI

BROADENING OUR PERSPECTIVE

When we add this depth of perception to our daily lives, our personal, social and business activities take on an altogether different character. We may begin to discover that to feel truly fulfilled we need to work towards the common good rather than focusing primarily on our own self-interest. We may also come to realize that our thoughts and actions have a collective impact as well as an individual outcome, that all aspects of human endeavor contribute ultimately to a much broader spectrum of awareness which finally transcends the efforts of any particular individual. From this broader viewpoint we can finally recognize a shared sense of purpose for all human beings upon Earth. This recognition often brings with it the feeling that each of us must undergo a process of personal transformation in order to assist both ourselves and the planet.

Once we commit to the work of transformation – a path which reflects our true nature and purpose – our lives begin to mirror this spiritual orientation. Of course, this is much easier said than done. Sometimes, for example, out of sheer necessity, we may find that we have to work in an area that is not of our own choosing or preference. Then, in order to hold onto our belief that we are capable of making a worthwhile contribution, we have to somehow develop a sense of purpose and commitment, regardless of the obstacles we may experience along the way. Nevertheless, if we bring a positive attitude to our situation, we may discover that these "obstacles" can become opportunities for personal growth and exploration.

Unfortunately most of us are not taught in school that challenges help us to grow and that apparent obstacles can become opportunities. It is largely left to young people – and also to their parents, most of whom are not trained in the processes of self-development – to discover this for themselves. The unfortunate result is that many people live their lives without realizing their true purpose and so they remain fundamentally discontented with the work they are doing. By the time they have gathered the means to be able to do something effective in their lives, the desire to accomplish something truly meaningful has waned. This is a real tragedy because until we can discover our true purpose in life, we will remain lost, restless and lacking in direction.

It is a great drawback that in spite of our widely held notions of "progress" so many individuals often have no opportunity to accomplish something they truly desire. This means that hundreds of thousands of lives are effectively wasted. And even those who do achieve high levels of material success may find that in spite of all

Whatever you can do

or dream you can,

Begin it.

Boldness has genius,

power and magic in it.

Begin it NOW.

JOHANN WOLFGANG VON GOETHE

the money they make and the benefits they acquire, in their hearts they are not truly satisfied. Many discover that material wealth, in itself, does not provide lasting satisfaction or real happiness.

PURPOSE AND HOPE

Motivational writer Dr. David Reynolds has proposed three basic guidelines for living: *Accept your feelings. Know your purpose. And do what needs to be done.* Here the actions to be undertaken have to be in line with your individual purpose, despite any feelings that may arise at any given time.

There is much to be learned from this advice. However, it is not always easy to know one's purpose in life so we may need to seek assistance that will bring clarity to this issue. Clearly, if we are to discover a true sense of meaning in our lives, we have to focus on what we really want to achieve. We then need to sustain that vision of our purpose in life and align our subsequent thoughts and actions with the nature of our personal resolve. We have to be truly able to achieve what we are hoping to attain.

But what do we mean by hope? One answer could be that hope is what we aspire to. However, hope is more than individual aspiration. Aspiration means achieving something just for ourselves, whereas the concept of hope is both wider and deeper – and takes personal effectiveness into a broader context. Hope can instill confidence in us – and provide us with a sense of empowerment which enables us to bring about change, both in our own life and also in society.

Hope may involve facing a wide range of issues that confront us on a daily basis. We may have to face our most deeply held fears or confront the sense of turmoil that seems to be engulfing us. We may have to identify specific life issues that we want to change, and develop a step-by-step plan to implement these changes. We may even have to face our own mortality – do we have enough time to achieve what it is that we have set out to do? Part of this process may also involve slowing down a little in order to acquire a greater sense of focus and to concentrate on the things that really matter. We may have to take some time out to deal with matters relating to healing, forgiveness or the acceptance of others. We may need to learn how to relax or meditate in order to discover the depths that lie within …

Hoping for something worthwhile certainly helps us to rise above the feeling that we are stuck in our present situation. It provides an impetus for us to move forward and gain some sense of control over our lives. Having the hope that positive and meaningful things can be achieved is clearly much more worthwhile than remaining stuck

The secret of life is the desire to attain something; the absence of this makes life useless. Hope is the sustenance of life; hope comes from the desire of attaining something. Therefore this desire is in itself a very great power. The object which a person wishes to attain may be small compared with the power he develops in the process of attainment.

HAZRAT INAYAT KHAN

in the belief that one's present situation is all there is. Hope provides us with the clear possibility of a way forward.

Nevertheless, hope has to be more than a simple wish list. Our aims have to be potentially attainable. We have to know within ourselves that we have the ability to bring about change and that this change will be positive both for the quality of our personal relationships and also for the community as a whole. After all, these changes may even have a positive impact on the lives and welfare of future generations.

Hope is invariably linked to such human values as trust, honesty, loyalty and love. In troubled times a sense of hope may also be associated with a desire for economic security and employment. In difficult situations we need to know who and what we can rely on. However, hope can also be closely tied to fear so we need to carefully examine what we are attaching our hope to. For example, Hitler gave the people of Germany a great sense of hope prior to the outbreak of World War II, but this investment of hope came at a horrendous cost. Hope is most effective when it embraces such universal values as joy, integrity, harmony, fulfillment and well-being – that is to say, when it encompasses true quality of life.

Follow your bliss.
If you follow your bliss, you put
yourself on a kind of track, which
has been there all the while
waiting for you, and the life
that you ought to be living is
the one you are living.

JOSEPH CAMPBELL

THE POWER OF BELIEF

Our beliefs are powerful motivators and also help us to define what we hope to achieve. They can also serve as a framework of self-definition, as well as providing a lens through which we relate to other people and daily life. So we need to be able to explore the nature of our beliefs and to ask ourselves honestly whether these beliefs are holding us back or showing us a way forward. Before we can change anything in our lives, we first have to face the present situation *as it actually is*. Only after we have done this can we set about the process of change – and this in turn may require a commitment that involves sustained perseverance. It also helps if one can lighten the load a little by regarding change as a challenge rather than a burden. A sense of optimistic acceptance can help us to make constructive changes in our lives, in ways that lead towards positive outcomes. It is important to remember, though, that our dreams – our optimistic hopes for the future – need to be realistic. This means dealing with life as it really is, rather than reconstructing it in an evasive, idealistic or utopian way to reinforce our fantasies about "what might be." Unrealistic hopes relating to unattainable alternatives invariably lead to a restless and unfulfilled state of being – wherever we are and with whatever we have.

When we live in the bliss, there is no difficulty that is insurmountable. If we miss the bliss, there is no compensation that is adequate. The highest order of duty to self is to follow your bliss … The highest order of duty to society is to make your fullest contribution to its well-being.

These duties meet in life's work.

LAURENCE G. BOLDT

SIMPLICITY, STILLNESS
AND MEDITATION

Although it may seem like familiar advice, these additional points are also worth making: *take time to be in Nature*. It is very nourishing to reconnect on a regular basis with the natural world – and it makes a pleasant and therapeutic change from the world of high technology and urban intensity. Take time out to reflect on the fact that if there is to be any hope for the future of humanity – and indeed for Earth itself and all of her creatures – we need to preserve our precious resources of clean air, clean water and a healthy food chain, and we need to keep our environment as free as possible from contamination.

It is also worthwhile to develop a capacity for simple joys and simple pleasures, and to develop a capacity to be still in order to discover our true self. This helps us to achieve a balance between *doing* and *being*. We are all too often busy with our aspirations, our work, our appetites and our addictions that so much passes us by without us even noticing. So it is important to take time and space to care for ourselves as well as for others, and to nurture the "soul" aspects of our everyday lives. This may involve developing some form of creative expression that enables us to express our innermost feelings. Meditation is a simple yet powerful method of inner unfolding – studies on meditation have shown that when people get together to simply meditate, without focusing on any specific outcome, their lives improve for the better.

Similar results have occurred with undirected prayer – this is making a simple prayer without specifying a desired outcome, and without asking or telling the Universe what to do. These approaches are ways of surrendering to the will of the Universe for the greater good, rather than imposing our will and desires onto life.

And it is also important to clear out the clutter from our lives – emotionally as well as physically. This will eventually "open" some extra space for our relationships with others, for the environment as a whole, and for new elements to enter our lives. If we are feeling hopeless we tend to close in on ourselves, and when we do this we are not contributing to either our own welfare or to society. Hope, on the other hand, gives us new life. Hope provides us with a sense of renewal which releases essential energy that enables us to act – both for ourselves and for others. Most importantly, hope provides us with a sense of meaning and purpose and helps us attain true quality of life. This in itself is one of the most wondrous simple pleasures we can experience as human beings.

Whether or not you know your ultimate purpose, or even your goals for next year, you almost certainly have a clear sense of what you want to do in the next few minutes. When the future is hazy, you can still handle what's in front of you. Destiny has a way of dropping a trail of bread crumbs – one small goal at a time – to mark the path. By paying attention to each day, each moment, you will see what needs to be done right now. Your immediate goals are the bread crumbs leading you toward what you cannot yet see.

Dan Millman

Most of us achieve only at rare moments a clear realization of the fact that they have never tasted the fulfillment of existence, that their life does not participate in true, fulfilled existence. We nevertheless feel the deficiency at every moment, and in some measure strive to find – somewhere – what we are seeking. Somewhere, in some province of the world or of the mind, except where we stand, where we have been *set* – but it is there and nowhere else that the treasure can be found.

MARTIN BUBER

"Come to the edge," he said.

They said, "We are afraid."

"Come to the edge," he said.

They came.

He pushed them …

And they flew.

GUILLAUME APOLLINAIRE

Fear and Courage

CONFRONTING FEAR

We only have to switch on our television sets or radios to be bombarded with news that is deeply unsettling. Maybe the news of the day focuses on widespread floods, drought or the ravages of forest fires? Or a major corporate collapse triggered by financial greed or corruption? Perhaps a new terrorist attack has been mounted against a group of innocent civilians with tragic and unforeseen consequences. Maybe we see images of starving children and people ravaged by disease. Perhaps we hear statistics of rising unemployment. Or there may be renewed warnings from government officials concerning the hostile use of biological weapons by nations perceived as potential enemies. It would seem that our lives are now continually assailed with threats or warnings of hostility which have the potential to undermine the very structure and security of our everyday existence.

When you undergo times of difficulty, it is necessary to sit back and wait. Don't act … There have been no great saintly people who have not experienced the darkness [of temptations and of not knowing how things will turn out] … We all have to go through a desert, even Jesus went through the desert for forty days. Let's remember that. Let's not have superhuman expectations. We become superhuman only by meeting the demands in the proper sense of not giving up. Even if you have to hold on by your teeth, your fingertips, or your toenails – just hold on. Wait.

SWAMI SIVANANDA RADHA

And while images of attack, deprivation or devastation may pour forth from the media on a regular basis, what about bad news or personal troubles much closer to home? Perhaps we fear losing what we already have, such as our income or our personal possessions? Maybe we face particularly difficult times at work that may result in us losing our jobs? Maybe something has happened which will cause us to fear shame or criticism? Perhaps we have been subjected to personal abuse or attack, or fear that we might be rejected or abandoned by a partner or some other family member? Maybe someone dear to us has just died, and this leaves us not only with a profound sense of personal loss but also with the feeling that our sense of emotional and financial security is crumbling?

In such circumstances it is quite understandable that we should become fearful. Indeed, at different times fear seems to descend on us from all fronts, whether it comes from the possibility of war or some other deeply unsettling events in national and international politics, or whether it arises through our work or personal relationships. Fear can also arise in us when we encounter strangers in unexpected circumstances, and sometimes even when we watch movies!

Some commentators believe that we are now experiencing an epidemic of fear that has reached global proportions. After all, fears aren't limited just to individuals. Fears can grip whole countries as well as specific towns and communities, corporations and businesses. We are then faced with dealing with widespread collective fear as well as fear held by the individual.

Nevertheless, individual fears are something which we all have to wrestle with at various times. These can take the forms of phobias, panic attacks, anxieties and insecurities about everything from fear of failure, fear of strangers or fear of traveling alone at night through to unexpressed fears which may later manifest in our bodies as the basis of psychosomatic disease and stress-related illness. And there seems to be widespread fear about facing our inevitable mortality.

Clearly, circumstances that have the potential to cause fear have become a constant in our lives. Nevertheless, there are different ways to respond to our fear. Fear does not have to engulf us; instead, fear can become a challenge, and an opportunity for personal growth and understanding. As Susan Jeffers says, the challenge is to "feel the fear, and do it anyway."

One of the most important things we should remember in dealing with fear is that it has the potential to damage the relationships that would otherwise provide us with support in developing our courage to confront it. Fear erodes love and an inner sense of security. When we don't feel strong enough to face our fear, such anxiety gathers momentum inside us, feeds on itself and seems to penetrate into our very being. On the other hand, if we are able to face our fears, we may also be able to discover many of our unrealized potentials and our positive human qualities. In this way our fears can become a pathway towards personal transformation.

Many of us experience fear in the form of personal suffering. In these situations our first response is often to shield ourselves from this suffering by any means available. Some of us will hide or withdraw in some way, while others will become angry, apathetic or depressed. Some people begin to overeat or seek distractions from their fear by abusing tranquilizers, alcohol or other drugs. Some who fear abuse may try to please the person who is actually causing the abuse, in an attempt to prevent further pain or assault. Others become extremely aggressive in order to attack what they perceive, often erroneously, to be the source of their fear.

Although the circumstances will vary with each individual situation, fear can often make us become stuck. Our fear paralyzes us and our lives go on hold. However, what we do next can become very important. If we react to our situation negatively, we may begin to feel that the only way out of the predicament is to withdraw or attack – and this can involve anyone, real or imagined, who we feel is obstructing us. On the other hand, if we respond positively to our fear, we may find that we not only become less fearful, we can also engage in actions that help us to move through our own individual circumstances and to see things from a new perspective. Perhaps we can learn to look at our fears – including the source of perceived threat – from another angle? Maybe we can learn to turn our fears into positive situations so that the ruptures in our personal relationships can begin to heal?

After all, the alternative is far less favorable! If we hold on to our fears and allow them to direct our lives, this not only disempowers us but will just perpetuate more fear. This in turn can reinforce the feeling that we were justified in responding to our fear with retreat or aggression, and it will lead to a polarized personal existence where we see our lives in starkly black and white terms – and under never-ending potential attack from our "enemies."

We all have to learn to face our fears and penetrate the deepest darkness of our anxieties. On some level we need to learn to reach a perception of trust that allows us to see that there is some sort of message within the fear that can show us a path forward. Somewhere in our personal "darkness" we have to look for a message of hope that will lead to new insights into our situation and new ways of seeking harmony and reconciliation.

There is a saying that where there is fear there is power. Reverend Mary Murray Shelton has observed that when we come to regard

It isn't for the moment that
you are stuck that you need courage,
but for the long uphill climb back
to sanity and faith and security.

ANNE MORROW LINDBERGH

fear as a messenger, that perception is potentially capable of creating an appropriate new response to our personal situation and we become more resilient and innovative in seeking that response. On the other hand, when we deny and avoid fear, it becomes an "enemy," pursuing us relentlessly, and growing larger and larger until we face it and find out its message. When we allow fear to motivate us into some form of negative action, regardless of any other outcomes, it is always ourselves we hurt.

When we act defensively, the outcome is that we become more afraid rather than less fearful. These fears exhaust our potential for creativity and narrow our personal focus. In short, our lives become smaller and more depleted rather than creative and enriched. On the other hand, when we proceed with whatever it is we are afraid to do or to be – despite our fears – more often than not we discover that it is not only still possible to act but that we are also able to perform well. Our fear, anxiety and nervousness alone cannot prevent us from moving forward.

It is sometimes said that the key to dealing with fear is to find a sense of love and balance within ourselves. If we do this, we begin to regain our innate humanity and can discover feelings of compassion and connectedness that seemed to be absent in our lives. Working with our fears in this positive way can help us to find a new sense of purpose. When we face up to our fears, rather than trying to escape them, we discover ourselves anew. We are able once again to discover the love that lives within us.

DEVELOPING COURAGE

As we confront our various fears, we become free of the imprisoning effect they have on us. We gradually let go of the fear we have been holding onto, and new personal qualities begin to emerge. We now discover a tangible sense of freedom and peacefulness and very often also a sense of creativity and joy. And something else emerges as well – *a feeling of courage which enables us to face what lies ahead.*

As we increasingly learn to heed the message communicated to us through our fear, we come to realize that this is not a message based on aggression. Nor is it a call to retreat from moving forward on our path through life. More commonly the message alerts us to the fact that a particular path of action has to be followed because this is of special significance as part of our personal development. Usually, as we heed this message, we no longer allow fear to prevent us from attaining our goals and, at the same time, we no longer attack others because we think they are standing in our way. Instead we develop a sense of composure which allows us to take the first steps toward our

The next time you encounter fear, consider yourself lucky. This is where the courage comes in. Usually we think that brave people have no fear. The truth is that they are intimate with fear. When I was first married, my husband said I was one of the bravest people he knew. When I asked him why, he said because I was a complete coward but went ahead and did things anyhow.

PEMA CHÖDRÖN

immediate goals. We may still be on the lookout for potential loss or threats but in all probability we will discover that these perceptions are much less significant than the full-scale obstacles our fearful mind had anticipated. And we now find that we can put our courage to the test and move forward to address our particular fear. The true test of courage is not an absence of fear but acting in spite of feeling fearful.

Among the gifts that the message of fear can bring to us as we act courageously are such qualities as strength, resilience and integrity. It takes real courage to venture into the inner darkness and to confront our personal demons. But this is something that no-one else can do for us. Only we can face our own fears and make the journey through them.

In addition, each time we do this, our self-confidence and personal power increase many times over and we learn to trust our inner guidance – which really comes from the sacred depths of our being. At the same time it is quite likely that we will also discover that many, if not most, of our fears were based on illusion in the first place. Our personal courage allows us to overcome these illusions and to pursue a path of freedom and inspiration in making the choices that will guide our everyday lives from the present moment into the future.

STRENGTHENING THE SELF

Strengthening the self has many dimensions – physical, mental, emotional and spiritual – and these involve practices of various kinds that enable us to develop self-discipline. On a physical level we can develop our strength through a healthy diet and regular aerobic exercise, sporting activities, yoga or martial arts routines, and we should also take care to avoid situations that may be physically harmful. But physical strength is a means of support to developing mental, emotional and spiritual strength. Clearly, we need to discover a sense of self-acceptance because this will help to build confidence in our abilities and an understanding of our strengths and weaknesses. We have to confront our fears and weaknesses rather than give in to them, develop our powers of intuition or "inner knowing," open our hearts, and cultivate patience and acceptance of others. We have to learn to live with difference, develop a capacity for tolerance, accord others the same rights we accord ourselves, and forgive transgressions made against us. We also have to learn to awaken feelings of empathy and compassion in our relationships with other people. These themes form the core structure of this book.

A key to success, happiness and spiritual advancement – the act of strengthening the self in a spiritual sense – is the attainment of

The most central spiritual task
of our time is working with our fear ...
Fear contracts the soul ... To work in a
healthy way with fear, one must live in
close, conscious connection with soul life
and develop spirituality that is an
ordinary part of daily life.
Love is the antidote to fear.

ROBERT SARDELLO

"mastery." According to the Sufi teacher Hazrat Inayat Khan, there are three stages in attaining mastery: "The first stage is the attaining of self-control. And when self-control is gained, the second stage is to control all the influences that pull one away from the path which one wishes to take. And when one has been victorious in this second stage, then there is a third stage which is the control of conditions, of situations. When a person has attained mastery, it may be called an inner initiation."

According to Sufi tradition, every soul is here on earth in order to fulfill a specific purpose within the overall scheme of life. When a person reaches a state of mastery, from that moment onwards he or she is chosen by Providence to be used as an instrument in order to accomplish a certain purpose. Sufi devotees believe it is not necessary to renounce the everyday world and go into retreat. People can attend to their families, their businesses, their professional commitments and their duties in life while at the same time developing the inner spirit which is the true hallmark of personal mastery. Hazrat Inayat Khan used to say that the spirit of mastery is like a spark – by blowing continually upon it, it will grow into a blaze, and out of it a flame will rise.

Many great spiritual teachers have brought a similar message to humanity. According to legend, the Buddha's last words to his student monks were to "Be a light unto yourself." By this he meant that one should follow the spiritual teachings and practices but always also test them against the truth of one's own experience. Jesus said much the same thing when he proclaimed, "Behold, the kingdom of God is within you." This wise advice to seek "within" and become a "light unto yourself" is not only telling us *where* to seek, but also *how* to seek. This perennial wisdom teaching directs us to acknowledge and honor the sacredness that is within us all and to authentically cultivate the sacred purpose that is unique to each of us.

The essential message here is to be true to yourself at all times. Often, in our attempt to maintain a sense of "spiritual correctness" we tend to forget this teaching. We strive for the *idealism* of spiritual perfection – a spiritually correct posture of peacefulness and equanimity – but this fails to acknowledge our own unique human qualities, as well as the shadows of the past that invariably we all will have to deal with in life. We all have our individual personalities, and we all have our individual paths through life – as part of the evolutionary process that is continuously unfolding. Strengthening the self involves not only following the spiritual disciplines and teachings of the wisdom traditions but also requires that we heed the guidance from the unique inner voice that comes from within – guidance which arises from the sacred depths of the soul.

Our deepest fear is not that we are inadequate.

Our deepest fear is that we are powerful

beyond measure.

It is our light, not our darkness that most frightens us.

We ask ourselves, who am I to be brilliant, gorgeous,

talented and fabulous?

Actually, who are you not to be?

You are a child of God.

Your playing small doesn't serve the world.

There's nothing enlightened about shrinking

so that others won't feel insecure around you.

We were born to manifest the glory of God
that is within us.
It's not just in some of us – it's in everyone.

And as we let our own light shine, we unconsciously
give other people permission to do the same.
As we are liberated from our own fear, our presence
automatically liberates others.

MARIANNE WILLIAMSON,
SPOKEN BY NELSON MANDELA
IN HIS 1994 INAUGURAL ADDRESS

Birds make great sky-circles

of their freedom.

How do they learn it?

They fall, and falling,

they're given wings.

RUMI

FREEDOM AND RESPONSIBILITY

BEING FREE

We all cherish our freedom, but what does it really mean to be free? If we think that being free simply means being able to do what we want when we feel like doing it, more likely than not this will lead us towards acts of self-indulgence. Such an attitude would take little account of our relationships with other people and the way our thoughts or actions might impact on them. So when we consider the nature and expression of our own personal freedom we also have to explore the nature of responsibility. In expressing our right to freedom we have to ensure that our own freedom does not come at someone else's expense. Having said that, there can be no doubt that real freedom is a wonderful experience. As soon as we feel free within ourselves, our life has a renewed sense of energy and purpose. We feel a sense of well-being and that we are living life to its fullest. We also feel a deep inner peace and sense of equanimity and this, in turn, leads to feelings of happiness and contentment. True freedom is an inner state of being and ultimately comes from awakening to our true nature and from living authentically, irrespective of external conditions. This is not an easy state to attain and requires commitment and practice. It is particularly difficult to achieve when one's physical, emotional or psychological well-being is under threat.

In countries ruled by totalitarian governments – that is to say, in countries where people do not have freedom of expression or movement – we find a different sort of atmosphere entirely. Here, the right to express one's personal views is rigidly curtailed, the pursuit of personal happiness is accorded little significance, and feelings of suspicion, distrust and ill-ease abound as human rights are eroded. As the Dalai Lama has said, when a person's basic sense of trust is destroyed, how can we expect them to be happy? Two aspects of freedom are important here. We have to carefully consider and nurture those things that help to free us, and we also have to guard against those forces that have the potential to erode or restrict our own – and other people's – personal happiness and freedom.

FREEDOM AND PERSONAL EXPECTATIONS

Some people equate freedom with the idea of having total control over their own lives. However, contrary to what most of us have been taught or have come to believe, trying to gain control over every aspect of our lives is *not* the path to freedom, and not only is it impossible, it is based on erroneous expectations. Expectations, by their very nature, are all about becoming attached to a desire or a hope that people will do what we desire or that situations will turn out a certain way. However, while we may be able to influence certain outcomes in a superficial sense, no-one has total control over future events, so trying to control life sets up expectations that are doomed to fail. Building expectations also leads to self-sabotage and disappointment.

Significantly, building expectations also robs us of the freedom to see other options and to make other choices aligned to the actuality of changing circumstances. Having expectations of life and of others makes us dependent on outer circumstances for a sense of well-being, achievement and happiness. For this reason, the very act of having strong expectations can actually disempower us and diminish our sense of well-being and inner peace.

Never think in terms of being free from; always think in terms of being free for. Be free for God, be free for truth, but don't think that you want to be free from the crowd, free from the church, free from this and that. You may be able to go away one day, but you will never be free, never … Always remember not to throw the responsibility somewhere on someone else, because then you will never be free of "it." Deep down it is your responsibility.

OSHO

KARMA AND PERSONAL ATTACHMENT

The teachings of Buddhism can help us to understand the processes of having expectations and attachments. According to the Buddhist notion of karma, positive thoughts and actions produce positive outcomes, whereas negative thoughts and actions produce negative outcomes. Potentially, every action has a universal dimension and can impact on someone else's happiness. A sense of ethical responsibility is therefore very important if we are to ensure that our actions do not harm others. Developing our ethical awareness also reminds us of important spiritual qualities such as love, tolerance, compassion and humility. As we begin to embody these positive human qualities, we are less inclined to self-absorption and we pay more attention to the needs of other people. We are usually also much happier because, as we worry less about ourselves, our own suffering becomes less intense. Any disappointments, frustrations or anxieties we may have been feeling become increasingly less significant and our life takes on a renewed sense of vitality and aliveness.

All of this is very significant as we come to reflect on the nature of the problems that we may feel are dominating our lives. While Buddhism readily acknowledges that pain and suffering are part of everyday life, most problems, in themselves, are not the real concern.

It is our attachment to the issues and emotions associated with the problems that actually gives rise to our suffering. Buddhism teaches us that as soon as we are able to drop our attachment, the suffering falls away. Of course, this observation also has a strong bearing on how we regard our sense of personal freedom. As spiritual teacher Osho used to say, "If you want to be free, get out of your own way."

FACING OUR ADDICTIONS

In this troubled age, addictions of various kinds have reached pandemic proportions across the planet. Indeed, the worldwide incidence of addiction has never been greater or more destructive than it is now. There are many things that we have become addicted to; for example, drugs, alcohol, food, gambling, sex, violence, computer games, extreme dietary regimes … So why is it that we are raising this issue in relation to personal freedom? The answer is clear. When we are addicted to anything, we cannot be truly free.

If we are tempted to overeat excessively, or to abuse drugs or alcohol, what we are really doing is allowing ourselves to act irresponsibly. If we are unable to resist the impulse to indulge our temptations, we have become addicted – and we have in turn yielded our personal power and freedom to the particular addiction that now controls us. Well-known writer Gary Zukav has described addictions as "the wants of the parts of your personality that are very strong and resistant to the energy of the soul. They are those aspects of your personality, of your soul incarnate, that are most in need of healing. They are your greatest inadequacies." It may be that we have more than one addiction and that they are all working in tandem, thus taking a heavy personal toll on our lives. However, we cannot release ourselves from our addictions until we understand the nature of the dynamics that are driving them. Beneath every addiction, says Gary Zukav, is an issue of power.

Jungian analyst Marion Woodman has written extensively on addiction and says it is an unconscious way of avoiding pain. Today, pain is seen as something abnormal, a discomfort to be removed as quickly as possible – through any available means. However, in removing pain from awareness, we are removing ourselves from what the body–mind is trying to tell us. We are also removing ourselves from what pain can teach us. And we are choosing to deny a reality of life – that pain is an intrinsic aspect of human experience. This denial keeps us emotionally isolated and robs us of the opportunity to heal.

Irrespective of the source of our addiction, it remains true that we cannot begin to release ourselves from our addictions until we first acknowledge that we are actually addicted. Perhaps we rationalize our addictions away and make light of them, pretending that they are unimportant, or we lie to ourselves and to others in order to avoid making this acknowledgment. This, however, is a delusion. Until we face our addictions we cannot reduce the power they have over us, and we cannot be free. The answer to this is to explore those areas of our lives where, instead of facing our fears, anxieties and pain and taking responsibility for our lives, we allow circumstances to overtake us.

Perhaps in confronting our addictions we will have to face some of our most entrenched and deeply felt fears. We may also have to face some painful memories or unpalatable truths about ourselves that we have suppressed or kept hidden behind the constructed self-image we present to the world. Until we do this, we are not facing the truth about our lives and acknowledging the hold that our particular addiction has on us. Only when we confront our addictions head-on can we begin the process of healing and regain our sense of personal power and effectiveness. Only as we choose to consciously challenge our addictions, and commit to the difficult and joyful inner work of healing, can we move progressively and consciously towards a sense of wholeness. All of this demands that we become more responsible for our everyday actions. Learning to act responsibly

Basically, every human individual carries responsibility for the benefit or welfare of humanity and for the planet itself, because this planet is our only home. We have no alternative refuge. Therefore, everyone has the responsibility to care not only for our fellow human beings but also for insects, plants, animals, and this very planet, However, the initiative must come from individuals. But then, in order to make an impact, the unified mobilization of individual forces through various organizations is the only path ... Universal responsibility is the key to human survival. It is the best foundation for world peace.

HIS HOLINESS THE DALAI LAMA

brings with it a sense of true personal empowerment which, in turn, provides us with a greater sense of individual freedom.

ACTING RESPONSIBLY

We mentioned earlier that it is a good idea to rid ourselves of expectations or attachments to specific outcomes. However, there is nothing wrong in opting for certain preferences in everyday life. Indeed, becoming conscious of the choices you make is highly desirable. The first step is to become really aware of the choices you make each and every day. Behind what you choose, with each thought and each action, is an intention – a quality of consciousness – that you bring to each thought or action. As a general practice, it is helpful to learn to focus your conscious awareness on the thoughts and feelings involved in each act of choice-making.

When you have practiced this self-awareness for a while and are about to make a specific choice, focus your thoughts on the possible consequences of the particular choice you are considering. Ask yourself whether this choice is based on integrity and responsibility and is likely to engender understanding and positive outcomes to both yourself and also to those who may have to bear some of the consequences of the particular choice involved. However, it is important to realize that you will not be able to choose your intentions consciously until such time as you become fully aware of each of the different aspects of yourself.

Most of us have different parts to our personality with varying degrees of entrenched patterns of thought and behavior. Often, these different aspects compete to satisfy themselves, which can involve contradictory behavior. So if you are not conscious of each part of your personality, you will find yourself wanting to intend, to say, or to do something but find yourself intending, saying or doing something different. You may want your life to move in a particular direction, but find that it moves in quite another direction. Also, you may wish to release a repeatedly painful pattern from your life and yet see it reappear once again. This will remain the situation until such time as you become fully conscious and your fragmented personality becomes whole.

In becoming more consciously responsible, you may also wish to draw on your inner intuitive knowing in seeking a heartfelt response as to whether or not you are doing the appropriate thing. If your decision feels right to you – if you feel a positive energetic sense within – go ahead and proceed with your decision. If you don't receive some sense of inner accord that this feels the right thing to do, you may wish to pull back from acting on the particular choice which you were considering. More time may be needed for clarity to emerge around the appropriate direction to take. In both cases, however, you are acting in a responsible way. In adopting this approach, you are assuming ethical and moral responsibility for your thoughts and actions.

When something "bad" happens to us, often our first response is to blame someone or something else for what has occurred – so we become a "victim" of the adverse situation. Very often, though, such a response is unjustified, and really represents an attempt to avoid taking full responsibility for our own actions. And we all have to face the fact that accidents and unfortunate experiences are a part of life.

As contemporary life continues to move at an ever more demanding pace, and many of us experience greater pressure in our work places and domestic situations, it is easy for us to blame external factors for our seeming misfortunes. Hardly surprisingly, more and more people now rush to engage themselves in lengthy and expensive legal confrontations – suing others whom they blame for their own adverse circumstances. Sometimes this may be justified, but frequently it is not. In such situations many of us have a tendency to project onto others our own feelings of anger, insecurity, aggression, depression, hostility, intolerance, impatience and unhappiness – when, in fact, *no-one* other than ourselves is actually responsible for how we feel.

Sometimes people can behave unkindly towards us, as we can behave unkindly towards them, but we are still responsible for how we choose to respond. If we fail to think and act responsibly when we experience setbacks, and we reactively blame others for causing our problems, more often than not we are failing to face up to the realities of life. Undoubtedly, painful things happen to "good" and "bad" people alike, but when such difficulties occur we still need to take the responsibility to look calmly and dispassionately at ourselves and the situation before rushing to blame others for what has occurred. Usually, we need a little time for our emotions to settle and to consider an appropriate response.

In his thoughtful book, *The Deeper Wound*, Deepak Chopra suggests an exercise that can be done on a regular basis. It is a practice that involves not clinging to anything for a whole day. "Not clinging" means accepting whatever happens without protest or resistance. Through acceptance you make yourself available. Acceptance puts other people at ease, which in turn makes love possible. If you are full and complete in yourself, if you lack nothing, if your desires come and go easily, you will always be free. In this freedom there is total joy. You cannot be hurt, not in your true self. This is a lesson worth heeding as we seek to avoid blaming something or someone external to ourselves for our misfortunes.

The dynamic beneath all addictions is the desire to prey upon a soul that is more shattered than oneself. This is as ugly to look at as it is to experience, but it is the central core of negativity within our species ... Humbleness, forgiveness, clarity and love are the dynamics of freedom. They are the foundations of authentic power.

GARY ZUKAV

We who lived in concentration camps can remember the men who walked through the huts comforting others, giving away their last piece of bread. They may have been few in number, but they offer sufficient proof that everything can be taken from a man but one thing: the last of the human freedoms – to choose one's attitude in any given set of circumstances …

VICTOR FRANKL

Have we not come to such an impasse
in the modern world that we must love
our enemies – or else?
The chain reaction of evil –
hate begetting hate,
wars producing more wars –
must be broken, or else
we shall be plunged into the dark abyss
of annihilation.

MARTIN LUTHER KING, JR.

GOOD AND EVIL

Good and evil are widely regarded as the basic polarities of everyday experience. And although we all have our own individual definitions of what we mean by "good" and "evil," we may also think immediately of specific people or circumstances that, for us, embody these characteristics. For example, when we reflect on highly evolved human qualities, our minds may turn to influential contemporary figures such as Mother Teresa, and Nobel Peace Prize winners such as His Holiness the fourteenth Dalai Lama, Nelson Mandela or Burma's democratically elected leader Aung San Suu Kyi – all of whom have been a profound force for good in the world. On the other hand, when we consider dark episodes in human history and reflect on certain individuals whose actions have unleashed extreme brutality, death, destruction and misery on a vast scale, figures such as Adolf Hitler, Joseph Stalin or Pol Pot – creator of the notorious "Killing Fields" in Cambodia – come immediately to mind.

GOOD

We recognize a saint as a person who puts aside self-centered concerns in order to selflessly serve humanity, and most of us can readily distinguish this type of person from a tyrant who engages in acts of barbarism, cruelty and treachery. However this is a contrast of extremes. We can also distinguish between good and evil, or positive and negative, in a more general way.

Most of us appreciate the basic distinctions between love and hate, creation and destruction, peace and chaos, benevolence and selfishness, charity and greed. Sometimes the qualities that we believe are fundamentally "good" are more easily recognized by contrasting them against their negative counterparts.

But what do we really mean when we consider something "good?" What do we have in mind when we say someone is a "good" person? Although, on the surface, this may seem to be an easy question to answer, when we reach a little deeper we may begin to appreciate the complexity involved in arriving at such a definition. There are a few universal understandings – recognizing a person who is kind to others, one who is generous, who has integrity, who is loving, respectful, forgiving and tolerant, empathic or compassionate, and so on – yet the actual idea of what we perceive as "good" or "bad" can also be strongly influenced by our cultural or religious beliefs.

We may refer to a person who does good works as a "good" person without really knowing whether that person's motivation is based on self-interest or on a genuine intention to help others. Similarly, a person who appears to have done something "bad" may have been motivated by good intentions. So there is always a possibility that "good" people may have done "bad" things and vice-versa. For these reasons, it is always unwise to judge others without first examining honestly one's own life in order to understand the many layers and complexities that constitute the ongoing struggle between the so-called "good" and "bad" within ourselves.

So what is genuinely good in human nature? As we have already mentioned, the qualities generally associated with goodness are sincerity, kindness, generosity of spirit, integrity, tolerance, respect, empathy and compassion. To these we could add a peaceable disposition, a capacity to make personal sacrifices for the welfare of others, unconditional love, and humility. These qualities emerge in someone who feels a genuine sense of equality and benevolence towards all sentient beings and to Nature generally. A true sense of equality makes no distinctions between people on the basis of superficial differences, such as race or cultural group, gender, religious belief, age and so on. People who genuinely embody a sense of

There is nothing either good or bad,

but thinking makes it so.

WILLIAM SHAKESPEARE

equality do not distinguish between themselves and others in any sense of entitlement, and follow the precepts to do no harm and to treat all others as deserving of respect. In such ways does true humility emerge.

Lama Surya Das has written that, the world over, a person with a "good heart" refers to someone who is compassionate and who has a loving, caring and generous spirit. In the Tibetan language, the concept of compassion is perceived as nobility or greatness of heart and includes open-hearted wisdom and discernment as well as empathy and unselfishness. It also refers to a capacity for abundant loving kindness towards others.

Some of us may feel that attaining a state of consistent loving kindness towards all sentient beings is fundamentally out of reach for most people. But it is just a matter of degree. Every act of human kindness makes the world a better place to live in. Every human being who is touched by kindness will in turn reach out to touch other lives in different ways. We do not have to become sages or spiritual leaders in order to bring qualities of kindness, tolerance and compassion into our daily lives. Many believe today that the collective healing of this suffering world can only come about through each of us making a personal commitment to embody those qualities we consider "good" and to bring them forth into everyday life.

EVIL

Many fundamentalist devotees of the mainstream Western religions – Christianity, Judaism and Islam – believe that the force of evil takes the form of a supernatural being known as Satan or the Devil, and that this being stalks humanity looking for endless opportunities to wreak havoc and destruction in the world. From this perspective, life itself then becomes a type of battleground between God and Satan and human beings are caught up in the eternal conflict between them.

Some religious followers who espouse deeply held beliefs find no difficulty at all in overriding the core biblical teaching "Thou shalt not kill" if they believe their enemies are evil. President of the United States, George W. Bush, a committed Christian, has expressed the view that certain political regimes – specifically those in Iraq, Iran and North Korea – represent an "Axis of Evil" because they pose a major terrorist threat to the United States through their accumulation of weapons of mass destruction. This view does not take into account the fact that many Western countries themselves hold vast stocks of weapons of mass destruction. Indeed, several leading Western governments have sold lethal weapons and provided military training to those same governments now branded as "evil."

Good and evil are polarities.

When we say a person falls prey to evil

we mean a person who has taken leave of

his senses, who has fallen prey to his

passions, his vice, selfishness, falsehood,

vanity, lust, greed and fanaticism.

RUTH NANDA ANSHEN

Similarly, terrorists intent on attacking America – a country perceived by some fundamentalists as the Great Satan – make no distinction whatever between any American citizens: they are all regarded collectively as "the enemy" and each individual citizen in turn becomes a potential target. In such situations where religious dogma overrides ethical behavior, doing something normally considered "bad" – such as harming or killing people – can then come to be considered "good." Among fundamentalist Muslims, for example, a *jihad*, or religious war, is a noble cause and its martyrs will be rewarded in Paradise.

So what do we mean when we refer to someone as evil? According to Ruth Nanda Anshen, "When we say a person falls prey to evil, we mean a person who has taken leave of his senses, who has fallen prey to his passions, his vice, selfishness, falsehood, vanity, lust, greed and fanaticism." Terrorist attacks which target unsuspecting civilians, but which are intended as actions against a government's hostile or exploitative political policies, are regarded as examples of politically motivated evil. Yet, most people like to believe that they have good – or God – on their side and that it is their adversary who is evil. But this doesn't answer what many consider to be a really important question: Is evil something that is external to us, or is it the embodiment of dark, hostile, unresolved issues which lurk within us

When I see an erring man I say to myself,

I have also erred;

when I see a lustful man I say to myself,

so was I once;

and in this way I feel a kinship with

everyone in the world,

and feel that I cannot be happy without

the humblest of us being happy.

MAHATMA GANDHI

all and which we then project out onto the world? As William Shakespeare expressed in *Hamlet*, "There is nothing either good or bad, but thinking makes it so."

M. Scott Peck, best known for his famous book *The Road Less Traveled*, notes in a more recent work, *People of the Lie*, that one characteristic of evil people is that they inflict their own pain, inadequacy and imperfection onto others through projection and scapegoating: "They themselves may not suffer, but those around them do." Peck also thinks that evil people are driven by fear. "They are terrified that they will be exposed to the world and to themselves. They are continually frightened that they will come face-to-face with their own evil."

One writer who believed that evil was a potentiality of the human psyche was the late Joseph Campbell, a well-known scholar in the field of comparative mythology. Campbell's special skill was his ability to relate the themes of mythology to the human condition. Campbell did not believe that gods or devils exist in a literal sense but regarded them instead as archetypal expressions of our own inner being. According to Campbell, "Your god is a manifestation of your own level of consciousness. All of the heavens and all of the hells are within you ..." Campbell believed that we all carry evil within ourselves. The famous psychologist Carl Jung – a major influence on Campbell – referred to this inner darkness as our "shadow" – unconscious aspects of ourselves which exert a powerful influence on our lives. According to Jung's perspective, one of our key tasks in becoming balanced and "whole" human beings is to identify our shadow, develop a relationship or dialogue with it, and then integrate its transformed state into our being. Essentially, we need to confront and "own" the dark parts of ourselves that we find unacceptable and fear, and do not want to acknowledge. When we are prepared to look within and face the darkness within ourselves, and acknowledge both its power and also its weakness, we can then begin to bring that darkness into the light of awareness where it has less influence on our psyche.

KINDNESS

Let us now consider the different responses we might make towards acts of goodness as compared to acts of hostility or aggression. When someone demonstrates kindness, we find ourselves responding to them with greater openness and trust. Giving and receiving acts of kindness develops a sense of warmth and connection between individuals and helps people to appreciate each other. Acts of kindness can also be extended to strangers. Being kind to someone

In the world of duality sooner or later everything must turn into its opposite. Day becomes night. Living things die. Good fortune turns to bad fortune. Good fortune deceives us into investing our happiness in necessarily transitory appearances, which must ultimately disappoint. What appears to be bad fortune, on the other hand, can inspire us to seek out a deeper source of joy by discovering the perpetual bliss of our permanent essence. The apparent evils of life are the Good in disguise.

TIMOTHY FREKE AND PETER GANDY

you don't know may appear to be less rewarding than being kind to someone you do know, but acting kindly to a stranger nevertheless represents an expression of your awareness that other human lives also matter.

Although there are times when the world seems disturbed by hostility and violence at present, most human beings prefer peace, cooperation and tranquility to negativity and aggression. As many mothers will attest, young babies respond best to a smiling face and a loving touch – so, clearly, acts of kindness have a naturally positive impact on human development. As young children learn to play with each other, they also discover the pleasure and the necessity of cooperation in developing mutual trust. Sadly, this sense of cooperation and connectedness seems to dissipate as we get older and as we become increasingly encultured by the aggressive and competitive norms of adult society.

We may even come to believe that human nature is innately violent and aggressive. Indeed, this is a view that is implicitly conveyed to us through media reportage as well as through the plethora of violent action movies and computer games. And yet if we continue to divide the world into pockets of good and evil, in the way seen so often in contemporary international politics and in different media, we are unlikely to create harmonious societies –

Within the wide arena of everyday
life we see evil in all of its ugly dimensions.
We see it expressed in tragic lust and inordinate
selfishness. We see it in high places where men
are willing to sacrifice truth on the altars of their
self-interest. We see it in imperialistic nations
crushing other people with the battering rams of
social injustice. We see it clothed in the garments
of calamitous wars which leave men and nations
morally and physically bankrupt.

MARTIN LUTHER KING, JR.

either now or in the future. Obviously, those who feel threatened generally do not feel motivated to extend goodwill to those who threaten them and so mistrust and aggression continue to reverberate around the world. This is something very apparent from a study of history and also pertains to current trouble spots such as Israel and Palestine, Afghanistan, Pakistan, Iraq and Africa.

And yet, clearly, acts of hostility and aggression – as well as branding the perpetrator as an enemy or "evil-doer" – are not the only options available to us. It is surely worth reflecting on the fact that acts of kindness and generosity are uplifting to the human spirit. As psychotherapist Stephanie Dowrick has written, "Every act of generosity – the willing giving of your time, interest, concern, care, understanding, humor, loyalty, honesty – expresses and nourishes love. And every missed opportunity to be generous erodes your experience of love, connectedness and spirit."

Everyone carries a shadow,
and the less it is embodied in the
individual's conscious life,
the blacker and denser it is.

CARL JUNG

The reality of evil is a well-kept secret,

guarded by the dark forces themselves;

for they thrive on concealment …

The power of Light increases as it is

brought to consciousness.

Darkness loses its power when revealed.

PATRICIA JOUDRY AND MAURIE D. PRESSMAN

Love is the way messengers

From the mystery tell us things.

Love is the mother

We are her children.

She shines inside us,

visible-invisible,

as we trust or lose trust,

or feel it start to grow again.

Rumi

Love, Compassion and Forgiveness

LOVE

Love, it is said, makes the world go around. At our core, we are beings of love. We are, in truth, spiritual beings having a human experience. An intrinsic aspect of that experience is the search for love. Whether we are aware of it or not, all of us are searching for love. Without love we are lost. And sadly, the world today seems to be very much lacking the presence of love.

Most of us have been brought up to believe that love is to be found somewhere "out there" – initially in our parents and later perhaps in a special person who is destined to become our lover or soul mate. Perhaps this special person will also become our wife, husband or partner? On "finding" this particular person we are

There is nothing better than love.
It feels good because it is the Good.
Love is what happens when we connect
deeply with another sentient being
because love is the way we experience
the mysterious paradox of being
the One appearing to be many.

TIMOTHY FREKE AND PETER GANDY

deemed to have, at last, "found" true love. And, we are led to believe, our yearning for love will now be fulfilled.

But there is an additional dimension to this quest for a special love. Many of us assume that when we have found our special partner, this love will last throughout our lives. We have not realized that people change, that couples can grow apart, that sometimes a partner leaves us or we leave them, and that both of us will eventually die, and not usually at the same time. We are yet to understand the transient nature of all forms of existence. And what about those on whom fate does not bestow loving parents, or a loving "mate?" Are they destined to remain loveless – always seeking, never finding? Or is there another dimension to love that can be "found" in life itself – within us all – guiding us towards discovering our true nature.

Some of us do "fall in love" and this is surely one of the most wonderful human experiences. When we are "in love" the whole world becomes an enchanted place – the boundaries between ourselves and the person we love appear to dissolve, and we feel intimately connected. It is as if we have entered a different, and quite remarkable, realm of awareness. Being in love momentarily transforms us – we experience a peak of happiness in a more intense and all-encompassing way than we have before. As long as we are held in its thrall, we feel truly alive through the power of love.

However, everything that rises up must someday fall. Inevitably, individual differences, expectations, social conditioning, the re-establishment of personal boundaries and our individual human foibles and weaknesses slowly – but sometimes quickly – enter into the relationship. We may now enter a phase of disappointment and disillusionment, accompanied by a lessening of our feelings of love. Our "love" may even turn to dislike. Cracks begin to appear in our projections. At this time we begin to come down from the "high" that we have associated with being in love with a particular person.

How do we deal with our feelings of disillusionment? What do we do? Should we endure, and hope that the magical feeling of the first rushes of passion will return? Should we continue to hope that our partner will change back to how we imagined them before? Should we consider changing our partner – like acquiring a new model car or some other updated commodity? Or do we commit to grounding our relationship in reality, to developing tolerance of difference, and to nurturing bonds of caring and friendship as well as intimacy.

Many of us have unwittingly bought the fantasy of romance expounded in films, advertising and popular novels. We have confused "romantic love," the mating instinct and attachment, with real love. All our dreams are not going to come true, all our problems are not going to magically disappear, all the answers to life's perplexing questions are not going to be solved: this love is not going to whisk us above the dreary, mundane aspects of life …

Sometimes we really do find a partner in love and external circumstances then pull us apart, but this is the exception rather than the rule. When this happens, grief is a natural response to the loss of a deep connection. The loss of our illusions can also bring deep grief – as well as an opportunity to awaken to the true nature of life and love. If we are fortunate, we will eventually discover that love is not only located "out there" but that it actually resides unceasingly within us – which enables us to know when it is genuinely there and when it is not. We may also discover that when external factors in our relationships change, we don't necessarily lose "love" itself.

In our quest for love we need to recognize that love is an independent power, it is not something localized in particular human beings. We all have love within us and it is a treasure to be nurtured in all of our relationships – on a daily basis. As Gary Zukav has written, "Love is not a passive state. It is an active force. It is the force of the soul … It brings harmony and an active interest in the well-being of others. It brings concern and care."

Love itself is a current of energy that is eternally present, whether we recognize it or not. Love is the true foundation of our being.

COMPASSION

Many spiritual traditions around the world emphasize compassion as a highly important human quality, but what does it mean to be truly compassionate in responding to others? Compassion encompasses love, affection, kindness, warm-heartedness and a true generosity of spirit. Being compassionate means actively reaching out to others. It involves feelings of empathy with those who are suffering or whom we perceive to be less fortunate than ourselves. Compassionate action also involves working with ourselves as much as with others.

According to Buddhist tradition, which has explicit teaching and practices for cultivating compassionate action, the first step in generating genuine compassion is to appreciate the true nature of suffering. The Dalai Lama has defined compassion in terms of a "state of mind that is non-violent, non-harming, and non-aggressive." The desire to eliminate suffering is the first step but expressing true compassion also involves a sense of commitment, responsibility and respect towards others. He suggests that in developing compassion "perhaps one could begin with the wish that oneself be free of suffering, and then take that natural feeling towards oneself and cultivate it, enhance it, and extend it out to include and embrace others."

A mind committed to compassion is like an ever-full reservoir; a constant resource of energy, determination, and kindness. It is like a seed which, when cultivated, gives rise to many other good qualities, such as forgiveness, tolerance, inner strength, and the confidence to overcome fear and insecurity. It is like an elixir; capable of transmuting many unhappy situations into a beneficial outcome. Therefore, the expression of love and compassion should not be limited to one's friends and family. Nor is compassion just the responsibility of clergy, health care, or social workers. It is the necessary business of every sector of the human community.

His Holiness The Dalai Lama

It is also worth mentioning that pity and compassion are by no means the same. It is one thing to pity someone who is suffering but quite another to compassionately respond to their situation. Pity implies a feeling of condescension, whereas true compassion is impartial and non-judgmental. Compassion is also different from sentimentality. People who burst into tears at the sight of people or animals suffering are not necessarily responding from empathy and such reactions may be based on quite different factors, such as internalized guilt or fear, rather than genuine compassion.

As well-known Buddhist teacher Pema Chödrön has said, "compassion isn't some kind of self-improvement project or ideal that we're trying to live up to" and relating to others compassionately is a genuine challenge. "Really communicating to the heart and being there for someone else – our child, spouse, parent, client, patient, or the homeless woman on the street – means not shutting down on that person, which means, first of all, not shutting down on ourselves. This means allowing ourselves to feel what we feel and not pushing it away. It means accepting every aspect of ourselves, even the parts we don't like."

This is not easy to achieve because in helping others, sooner or later we will be confronted with all of our own unresolved issues. What we reject externally is what we reject in ourselves. We need to actively keep our hearts and minds open – rather than fixating, judging, or holding on to any preconceived perceptions.

The Dalai Lama believes that there are two types of compassion. The first type includes an element of attachment – "the feeling of controlling someone, or loving someone so that person will love you back." This is really only a partial expression of compassion and is unstable because it is basically conditional. It can switch from feelings of love and concern to resentment or hatred if circumstances change or a disagreement arises. The second, and more genuine form of compassion is not sentimental or conditional and is based on the understanding that all human beings – including oneself – have a right to be happy and to overcome suffering. In this form of compassion we respond to the other person unconditionally, irrespective of whether they are perceived to be a "friend" or an "enemy." As the Dalai Lama emphasizes, "It is based on the other's fundamental rights rather than your own mental projection. Upon this basis, then, you will generate love and compassion. That's genuine compassion …"

The figure of Mother Teresa comes to mind when we think of someone well known for an eminently practical form of compassion devoid of sentimentality. The example of Mother Teresa teaches us that when we act out of concern for others, our behavior

Although I speak with the tongues of men and angels, if I don't love, I am just a brash trumpet or a tinkling bell. Even if I have the gift of prophesy and the faith to move mountains, if I don't love I am nothing. I may give everything I have to feed the poor, and my body to be burned, but if I don't love it won't benefit me at all.

ST. PAUL

is automatically positive, and the peace this creates in our own heart brings peace to everyone we associate with. In acting compassionately we bring peace to our family, peace to our friends, to the workplace, to the community and to the entire world …

BLAME

Blame is not compatible with compassion because it seeks to identify one person or a group of people as being "right" and another as being "wrong." In times of considerable tension, it is common for minority groups to be unjustly "blamed" or scapegoated for prevailing socio-economic problems. It is also common for political groups or even the leaders of countries to attack or scapegoat their opponents, branding their behavior as "wrong," while taking the view that they themselves are "right" in what they do or propose to do. Similar dynamics also operate frequently within families, especially when family members are in conflict with each other. We also frequently blame ourselves when something goes "wrong."

However, the very act of blaming others prevents us from communicating constructively with those we accuse. The blame itself becomes a barrier to any genuine communication. And it is worth remembering that projecting blame may also be something we are generating to help us to feel better, when really we are experiencing pain or guilt deep within ourselves. Blame prevents us from seeing ourselves, others and situations as they really are.

A proven response to this situation is to try to develop empathy, and to recover that sense of inner tenderness and sensitivity which will open up channels of communication towards whomever it is we are criticizing or blaming. As we dig deep within ourselves to uncover our own compassion, we are also trying to discover a point of genuine connection – a bridge to the other person. Then the blame can begin to recede and the healing can begin.

Writer and teacher Robert Sardello says that a common view of relationships is that when people experience things as being difficult, they translate it as "the relationship is not working." However, he says that, on the contrary, this is a signal that something *is* working. So an important approach in dealing with blame and conflict in relationships is to look first at ourselves. Instead of becoming angry or aggressive and reinforcing the belief that we are right and the other person is wrong, we can try to keep our hearts open and search for the middle ground in a spirit of non-judgmental communication. Only when we are open in this way will blame dissolve.

The key thing is not to turn that "other" person or persons – the focus of our rage or disappointment – into "the enemy." And as we

When we think with love, we are
literally co-creating with God. And when
we're not thinking with love, since only
love is real, then we're actually not
thinking at all. We're hallucinating.
And that's what this world is: a mass
hallucination, where fear seems
more real than love.

MARIANNE WILLIAMSON

seek to develop our empathy and sense of openness towards such people, our conduct will also become more considered and more ethical.

In recent times we have observed a spate of corporate collapses brought on by the greed of unscrupulous financial managers and the collusion of unethical accounting firms. We are also witnessing a worldwide epidemic of sexual abuse of children in families from all levels of the social spectrum as well as in some branches of the Christian clergy. There is an urgent need to address such soul-destroying deceit and duplicity – masked so often in the guise of respectability and assistance – and seek to rediscover our capacity for genuine and responsible care and kindness towards others.

Ethical behavior means not causing harm. It involves "walking our talk." It involves taking other people's rights and feelings into consideration – even, and especially, when they differ from our own perspectives. Only then can empathy emerge. We may even find that we are able to build this capacity for empathy into genuine feelings of love, compassion and happiness. This is surely something invaluable for all human beings to cultivate.

Love is the proof

that God exists.

SINCLAIR SWAIN

FORGIVENESS

Usually, when we think of forgiveness, we are thinking of forgiving someone else for a perceived harm or wrongdoing – either to ourselves or to someone we care about. However, forgiveness is as much about forgiving ourselves for our own perceived transgressions or weaknesses as it is about forgiving others. In fact, being able to forgive ourselves is essential if we aspire to forgive others. It is unlikely we will be able to truly forgive another person until we have experienced forgiving ourselves.

It is often said that the irritation, anger, hatred or intolerance we feel towards someone else is a projection of the anger, hatred or lack of acceptance we have towards ourselves. When we learn not to reject those aspects of ourselves we do not like, and when we learn not to shut down or turn away from situations we consider difficult or painful, we may then find we can become more tolerant of others. The same applies to forgiveness. We cannot forgive in another person something we cannot abide or forgive in ourselves.

Choosing to forgive is no easy task – it requires real commitment and focus and is something we may have to work on every day. For example, forgive the driver who will not give way to you and the person who pushes in front of you in a line. Forgive the waiter who is slow to serve you and the salesperson who is impatient and rude. The same daily practice is to be equally applied to forgiving yourself.

There are people in society who become callous and violent in their treatment of others because they were maltreated when they were children. However, there are other people who were raised with love and care who also behave selfishly and irresponsibly towards others and who are also capable of tyranny, sadism and brutality. One's background is not the sole criterion of how one behaves as an adult. Also, at times, we all experience hostility, fear, envy and other negative thoughts and emotions. If we understand that this is part of our shared human condition, it can perhaps make us less inclined to judge and condemn others. Perhaps then we may be able to honestly look at our own weaknesses and address them.

At various times most of us have unleashed our anger onto an innocent person when in fact we were hurt or angry with someone else. If we continue to indulge our rage in this way, we not only unjustly inflict pain on someone, but we risk harming the positive relationships on which we depend. On the other hand, if we practice daily acts of forgiveness we can bring harmony into our lives and stop wasting precious life energy on negativity. It is also important to remember that to forgive yourself and others is a choice. If you decide not to forgive yourself, someone else or a certain situation, it

Forgiveness is not an occasional act;

it is a permanent attitude.

MARTIN LUTHER KING, JR.

can be beneficial to explore why, and to look at other options that might improve your life until such time as you feel able to embrace forgiveness.

It also important to note that forgiving a harmful act does not mean you are condoning it. Forgiveness certainly does not mean exposing yourself to ongoing harm or danger. We all expect that in a just society proven wrongdoers who are apprehended will be dealt with through the processes of the law. The crucial point here is that all of us must always take responsibility for our own actions and attitudes, and we should take care not to cause harm to others even though taking revenge might appeal to us on certain occasions! Responding to a harmful act in like fashion – the old adage "an eye for an eye and a tooth for a tooth" – only takes us deeper into pain, and we then have to live with the fact that we have reacted as aggressively as those who have hurt us. True forgiveness is about letting go of the past.

People are often unreasonable, illogical, and self-centered; Forgive them anyway.

If you are kind, people may accuse you of selfish, ulterior motives; Be kind anyway.

If you are successful, you will win some false friends and some true enemies; Succeed anyway.

If you are honest and frank, people may cheat you; Be honest and frank anyway.

What you spend years building, someone could destroy overnight; Build anyway.

If you find serenity and happiness, they may
be jealous; Be happy anyway.

The good you do today, people will often forget
tomorrow; Do good anyway.

Give the world the best you have, and it may never be
enough; Give the world the best you've got anyway.

You see, in the final analysis, it is between
you and GOD.

It was never between you and them anyway.

MOTHER TERESA

The entire world is being
driven insane by this single phrase:
"My religion alone is true."

RAMAKRISHNA

TRUTH AND CONCEPTS OF GOD

TRUTH

In spiritual Reality there is only One Truth, the Truth of one's essentially Divine Nature – the true Self, or God. In awakening to one's true Nature, one awakens to Truth. In awakening, one directly realizes the underlying unity in all that is. There is no separate individuality, no divisions of consciousness, only a Oneness of Being. This is ultimate Truth. And it is this Truth that pervades all. It is this consciousness within us all which allows us to feel truth, to know truth – in a relative sense – in the world.

But to know truth, to feel truth, to become true – or authentic – we need to learn how to be still – to go within and to openly listen. Because truth today is hidden behind all manner of obstacles and closed doors, both within us and without, we need to relearn how to contact truth, to find truth. The ways to do this are to be still, to meditate and to cultivate what we call today our intuition – and to commit to this as a regular practice. It is this inner knowing that is a reliable guide to what is true in life, and that leads us ultimately to experience consummate Truth.

It is a fact of modern life that many of us have become increasingly dependent on our computers, the Internet and the media – that is, on external sources – to help us to obtain up-to-date information about our world and to connect with other people. However, high-tech communications, useful as they are, expose us to information overload. Also, much of the daily news information we see and hear is negative in content. We are all trying to connect with the world and with other people in our everyday lives, but many of the messages we are receiving tell us that the world "out there" is an increasingly unfriendly and dangerous place.

At the same time, the pace of our daily working lives is quickening. Many of us worry about whether we can keep up with the intense rate of change that contemporary society is imposing on us. Will we be left behind if we don't maintain the pace? Will we still have any value as human beings if we don't conform to society's expectations? Will our everyday world have any lasting meaning? In such a situation, we may reasonably ask, is it any wonder that so many people's physical and emotional lives are now in a state of confusion, fear and turmoil?

Amidst the daily barrage of media hype, distressing news reports and rapidly changing societal structures, how can we begin to know where the truth about ourselves and the world may be found? As writer Carol Adrienne has observed, "Because we are creatures of our conditioning, because we are taught to do what is expected of us, we think our answers will be found in the external world. We are used to taking our cues from external sources – advice from parents, spouses, friends, religious leaders, mentors, professional groups or union leaders – and playing by the rules of whatever community has authority over us." However, in order to discover what is really true and what action is required in a particular situation, we need to look within. Somewhere within the seeming chaos of the everyday external world we have to discover our inner knowing and guidance.

Clearly, we all need access to some form of guidance that carries its own sense of authenticity and integrity. This means trusting more in the wisdom of our own experience and heeding the voice of intuition – a form of direct inner knowing. It is a natural potential we all share and is not reserved for a privileged minority. Intuition can take us beyond the barrage of rapidly changing external factors into the calm inner world of direct experience. This is where we will find out what is really true. When developed with discernment, intuition provides reliable guidance on how we need to act ethically in our lives.

It is important to recognize, however, that truth has many facets. There are the beliefs and perceptions we hold in relation to the world and our individual lives – concepts we personally believe to be true – but there is also that level of truth, mentioned earlier, which transcends the individual. This is transpersonal or ultimate Truth – the experiential knowledge of God, Self-Realization, the Divine, the One Light that shines through All – or whatever one calls, or however one describes, ultimate Reality. As long as we only *think* we know God – for example, through a particular conceptual framework or belief system – it is inevitable that we will come to different conclusions in relation to what is really true and sacred.

As we can see from the history of religious wars, *jihads*, crusades and the medieval Inquisition, when major differences of religious interpretation become the basis of political conflict such differences invariably create immense suffering. Such conflicts are based fundamentally on the judgment that one religious teaching is "right" and another "wrong." However, those who have had direct experience of God – whatever the nature of their chosen spiritual

Your religion was written upon tablets of stone by the iron finger of your God so that you could not forget. The Red Man could never comprehend or remember it. Our religion is the traditions of our ancestors – the dreams of our old men, given them in the solemn hours of the night by the Great Spirit; and the visions of our sachems, and is written in the hearts of our people.

CHIEF SEATTLE

Three things cannot be long hidden:

the sun, the moon, and the truth.

BUDDHA

path – recognize the authenticity of a sacred or numinous experience when spoken about by people following different spiritual traditions. These "mystics" do not feel any sense of political, social or religious division, despite the different forms of expression used to describe such sacred experiences – they regard all such experiences as manifestations of the Divine.

It is important to realize that we are all operating from partial knowledge of what we take to be reality. We are only ever able to see part of the picture, and hear part of the story. We are also carrying baggage from the past, both from our personal experiences and what we have inherited from previous generations – familial and cultural. Every single one of us on this planet has a different perspective – a different "take" on how we see and make sense of what we experience around us. On the basis of these perceptions we decide what is "true" and this determines how we act.

When we understand this process, it is easy to understand how conflicts arise every moment of every day, in ways small and large, both within ourselves and in our relationships with others. If we truly want to know what is true, and experience the freedom that comes from knowing and acting in truth, there is no easy way out. We have to wrestle with our own inner demons and limitations, we need to learn to openly accept what "is," however unpalatable it may seem, and we have to renegotiate our relationships in the world. And, as said earlier, we need to learn how to be still and to really listen. As with undertaking all aspects of change, to make this task manageable and achievable, we need a step-by-step approach to practice. However, we also need to make the commitment, right now, to act.

The bridge between what we perceive as "personal" truth and authentic spiritual reality is provided through the experience of inner knowing. Truth, or authenticity, is something that is lived – it is not an abstraction or something "out there" waiting to be discovered. Concepts of truth or authenticity, when not grounded in personal experience, remain only constrictive intellectual constructs. They are rigid impositions on reality rather than revealed truth. Truth is received through the heart, through the soul, through intuition – that still, small voice within, that quick flash of knowing. However, to be able to utilize the gift of intuition, we have to clear out a lot of the inner clutter and the dark aspects of our psyches. If we fail to do this, we will still be looking at life through the foggy lenses of our egotistic needs, desires, projections, expectations and fixed belief systems. And, for intuition to be truly effective, we need to share our insights and unconditionally open ourselves to that deeper well within where Divine Truth itself eternally abides.

CONCEPTS OF GOD

Who or what is God? Generally, when we speak of God we are referring to the notion of ultimate Reality, the One that is God, Divine transcendence, or Self-Realization. God is the supreme Mystery – and yet also provides the very basis for our being. God is the Creator, the ultimate arbiter, the highest source of Truth, morality and knowledge in and beyond the universe. When the famous physicist Albert Einstein was asked what lies beyond infinity, he replied, "The face of God."

Different religious traditions conceive of God in different ways. Christians speak of "God the Father," Muslims refer to the One God – Al Ilah, or Allah, and Jews know their God through the unutterable sacred name JHVH – usually translated as Yahweh or Jehovah. Judaism, Christianity and Islam – the so-called "People of the Book" – have all adopted essentially patriarchal concepts of God. In the Upper Paleolithic and Neolithic eras of prehistory, which we are now discovering were more advanced than earlier believed, religion centered on the feminine power and the worship of a female deity as the creatress of life. As eminent archaeologist Marija Gimbutas has written, the pre-Indo-European culture of ancient Europe was "characterized by worship of a Goddess incarnating the creative

The inability to accept the truth of transciency creates a longing for permanence, which can never be. The shift in consciousness that is needed is therefore a shift away from this experience of ourselves as separate and independent towards one of recognizing our essential unity and interdependence with all things.

EDDIE AND DEBBIE SHAPIRO

principle as Source and Giver of All." The Goddess "also represents continuity of life as a perpetual regenerator, protectress and nourisher. In this culture, the male element, man and animal, represented spontaneous and life-stimulating – but not life-generating powers." Many people in modern society are also drawn to honoring the feminine aspects of the Divine. Goddess worshippers and Wiccans refer to the Universal Goddess as the Womb of the Universe. Indigenous cultures around the world revere the Earth as sacred and refer to Her as Mother. They also worship the One Great Spirit who is formless and pervades all forms of life.

Among the great Eastern spiritual traditions, which are more experientially based, Hinduism – which contains a diversity of spiritual paths – features a multiplicity of gods and goddesses. Each of these deities embodies different aspects of the feminine and masculine energetic principles of the Divine – and all of these deities are said to proceed ultimately from the eternal, absolute and ineffable Truth that transcends all boundaries, definitions and forms. Buddhism acknowledges the Buddha as "the enlightened one" but does not regard him as God. Buddhists adhere to the Buddha's teachings and practices – and test these practices through their own experience – on the path to enlightenment. However, they do not acknowledge a personal God or Goddess but rather a formless, ultimate reality which they call the Void (*sunya*). However, the Mahayana school of Buddhism – found in Tibet, Nepal, Japan and northern India – also places great emphasis on the special role of *Bodhisattvas*: Buddhas of compassion who have chosen to incarnate into the world for as many lifetimes as is necessary for the world to become free of suffering. These are great spiritual beings who are regarded as living embodiments of the highest spiritual principles. In Tibetan Buddhist tradition, the Dalai Lamas are considered to be Bodhisattvas.

For Christians, the path to salvation lies in accepting Jesus, the Son of God, and following the teachings of the scriptures. Muslims believe that Mohammed (or Muhammad) is the one true prophet of Allah and they are bound to following the prescribed Islamic practices known as *Din*, which include prayer, alms, fasting and the commitment to undertake a pilgrimage to Mecca at least once in one's lifetime. Hindus and Buddhists believe in the spiritual law of karma – the universal law of cause and effect – and maintain that after experiencing a succession of reincarnations, during which human beings learn the karmic lessons of life and learn to transcend the limitations of the sensory world, they are able to attain a state of spiritual liberation. In attaining this state of enlightenment – Self-Realization or Nirvana – the individual merges with the ultimate state of Reality, or Oneness, that lies beyond form.

Man's inner world is deeply disturbing.
He wrestles endlessly with the problems of
freedom and his own ultimate destiny and
meaning. He sways between the beautiful
and the monstrous, and he makes the
monstrous look true.

GARY ZUKAV

An essential and crucial difference between the religions of East and West is the specifically Western idea of an exclusive relationship with God. According to Jewish Zionists, the teachings of the Old Testament confirm that the Jewish people have been specially "chosen" by Yahweh, and that specific territories in the Holy Land are sacred to Him. Christians believe that the path to God can only be achieved through devotion to his son Jesus Christ, and it is through Christ alone that one may attain salvation. And while Muslims do not consider Mohammed the Son of God, he is nevertheless regarded as the sole prophet of Allah. Muslims acknowledge such figures as Jesus, Abraham and John the Baptist as spiritual leaders from an earlier time but maintain that Mohammed is the last of the 28 prophets sent by God to show humanity the true path of spiritual salvation.

Clearly, when we are considering spiritual paths to enlightenment or salvation, concepts of exclusivity create division and separation. The divisive politico-religious situation of the current Jewish–Palestinian conflict is a disturbing example such division and separation.

Spiritual arrogance by evangelical followers of any religion is extremely disturbing . There is an inevitable gulf between extremist viewpoints – whether in Christianity, Judaism or Islam – when the

Authenticity is one of the greatest values in life.
Nothing can be compared to it. In the old terminology,
authenticity is also called truth. The new terminology
calls it authenticity – which is better than truth, because
when we talk about truth, it seems like a thing, like a
phenomenon somewhere that you have to find ... It is
not something waiting for you. You have to be authentic,
only then is it there. You cannot discover it. You have to
create it continuously by being true. It is a dynamic
process. Truth means being truthful.

OSHO

followers of these religions believe they have truth on their side. No religion that believes it offers an exclusive path to salvation can consider another religion as its equal. Unless divisive dogmas are addressed, any chance for religious tolerance in the West is likely to be superficial at best.

In strong contrast to the evangelical approach, Buddhism has always adopted a universal perspective and continues to maintain an ongoing constructive dialogue with followers of other faiths in order to challenge notions of spiritual exclusivity. Buddhism opposes the concept of gods who protect only one people and gods whose power stops at certain frontiers. As the Dalai Lama has commented, "Whoever excludes others will find himself excluded in turn. Those who affirm that their god is the only God are doing something dangerous and pernicious because they are on the way to imposing their beliefs on others, by any means possible. And proclaiming themselves to be the chosen people is the worst of all."

The essence of religious tolerance involves accepting the diversity of religious and spiritual expression. In this lifetime – or, according to Buddhists and Hindus, perhaps in the next – we will all draw closer to discovering spiritual Truth. But we will find it in our own time and in our own way. As the great spiritual teacher Sri Aurobindo said, "Truth is a pathless land."

Nature has to do with the body.

Fate with the psyche.

Freedom with Consciousness.

None is absolute,

God alone is the absolute.

In Neolithic times and earlier in the Upper
Paleolithic, religion centered on the feminine
power ... Just as the female body was regarded as the
goddess creatress, so too the world was regarded as the
body of the goddess, constantly creating new life from
itself ... The Goddess is nature and earth itself,
pulsating with the seasons, bringing life in spring and
death in winter. She also represents continuity of life
as a perpetual regenerator, protectress, and nourisher.

MARIJA GIMBUTAS

God is immanent and formless.

He is pure being and pure consciousness …

Because of giving precedence to worldly things,

God appears to have receded to the background.

God does not reside in any place

other than the Heart, Be sure that the Heart is

the "Kingdom of God."

God is not only in the heart of all.

He is the prop of all. He is the source of all, their

abiding place and their end.

BHAGAVAN SRI RAMANA MAHARSHI

There is no death,

only a change of worlds.

CHIEF SEATTLE

LIFE, DEATH AND REBIRTH

Understanding more about the transition through life into death is perhaps the greatest remaining challenge in the study of human awareness. If we could find out more about the nature of dying, we would not only learn more about what to expect when we die, but we might also understand more about how we should live our lives on the planet.

Many people who fear death focus on the idea that death seems so final and absolute – a one-way pathway to oblivion. Understandably the very idea of passing into non-existence arouses a profound feeling of personal crisis. How does it feel to simply not exist anymore? We also know from experience that the passing of loved ones arouses deep feelings of loss and grief, and that the death of a family member can radically alter the lives of relatives left behind. In such circumstances, how could anything positive or worthwhile possibly emerge from the encounter with death?

However, there is another way of addressing this concern that does not focus on death as an ending but on death as a state of transition. A central issue we must consider here is whether our lives are primarily physical or spiritual in essence. What is more fundamentally real – our everyday physical identity or our core inner being?

All of the mainstream religions offer perspectives on an afterlife and such teachings provide considerable reassurance to many devotees and followers. However, as our everyday lives become ever more secular, many people who have not embraced a religious faith would prefer to learn about death through reports of actual human experiences rather than through teachings based on religious belief or dogma. Fortunately, the scientific and medical investigation of what is now referred to as the "near-death experience" is beginning to provide useful insights into the nature of death itself.

HOW DO WE DEFINE DEATH?

We usually define death as the absence of all visible signs of life – there is no heartbeat or respiration and brain-wave activity has apparently ceased. For all intents and purposes such a person is clinically dead. The issues we will consider here relate to the experiences of people who have been declared clinically dead but who have revived and then recounted their mystical and visionary experiences in an "out-of-body" state of awareness. Because these people didn't finally die after all, their visionary episodes are referred to as near-death experiences, or NDEs. They nevertheless provide us with the best scientifically based data on what may happen to us when we die, and to this extent they represent a potential meeting ground between the worlds of science and spirituality.

The term "near-death experience" was coined in 1975 by Dr. Raymond Moody, an American philosopher and teacher. In 1972, Dr. Moody began collecting anecdotal accounts of near-death incidents and his work has become a major catalyst and inspiration for others interested in NDEs. There have been several systematic research studies of the phenomenon since then – most of them in the United States, Britain and Australia. In 1980, psychologist Dr. Kenneth Ring published the first scientific study of NDEs – an important work based on more than one hundred interviews with medical subjects who had survived near-death. Since then, many similar studies have been published.

Dr. Moody and Dr. Ring and their international colleagues have found that almost universally the near-death experience is associated with feelings of peace, joy and serenity. Many people undergoing an NDE feel that their soul has separated from the body, and there is

We must live each day as if
it were the only one we had.

ELISABETH KUBLER-ROSS

often an experience of journeying through a tunnel towards either a transcendent dimension or a specific realm such as a celestial valley, garden or heavenly city. Here, the person enters a realm of light and beauty and often meets deceased relatives, spirits or "guides" – and sometimes even religious beings they identify as Jesus or "God."

One of the most fascinating things about near-death experiences is that they are basically similar in all cultures. Near-death experiences do not appear to be influenced by a person's nationality, social class, age, sex, educational level or occupation. They are also similar irrespective of whether one is a religious believer, an atheist or an agnostic. In other words, the NDE seems to be telling us about the process of dying itself and the various stages or transitions of human consciousness which might occur beyond bodily death.

WHAT HAPPENS DURING AN NDE?

It may be worthwhile at this point to quote a few brief but character-istic examples of what NDE subjects actually report, because here we gain fascinating insights about the visionary realm beyond death:
"I felt as though I was looking down at myself, as though I was way out here in space … I felt sort of separated. It was a wonderful feeling. It was marvelous. I felt very light and didn't know where I was … And then I

thought that something was happening to me … This wasn't night. I wasn't dreaming …"

"I felt myself being separated: my soul drawing apart from the physical being, was drawn upward seemingly to leave the earth … it reached a greater Spirit with whom there was a communion, producing a remarkable new relaxation and deep security."

"I went into this kind of feeling of ecstasy and just started moving outward energetically … and then I experienced a replay of all of my life … from my birth to the actual operation … it was like it was on a fast-forward video … people, places, everything … I could see a light … like a silver-white light … It was just massive darkness and then massive light."

Near-death experience researcher Dr. Melvin Morse reports that there are nine traits which are common in the NDE:

1. *A sense of being dead*, which many describe as the experience of being unfettered and totally themselves
2. *Peace and painlessness*, a consciousness of earthly surroundings while feeling detached from them
3. *Out-of-body experience*, being a spectator rather than an actor, hovering over one's own body

Death is the only certainty there is;
life itself is uncertain. If you want to be
more alive you have to live in uncertainty,
you have to move into the unknown. What
your life is like is what your death will be
like. If you live your life without fear,
welcoming the unknown, your death will be
without fear. You will embrace death like a
bridegroom embracing his beloved.

OSHO

4. *Tunnel experience*, a feeling of being sucked into a tunnel that has an exit
5. *People of light*, when one emerges from the tunnel into brilliance, where people glow from an inner light
6. *Being of light*, when one meets a being who glows, nourishes and loves
7. *Life review*, in which one personally experiences the joy and hurt that he or she caused others in life
8. *Reluctance to return* to one's earthly body
9. *Personality transformation*, with a new perspective and appreciation, and a sense of being connected to the universe.

Near-death experience research also suggests that what we generally regard as our essential sense of self – who we *really* are as aware human beings – depends more on our inner state of consciousness than on our external, physical identity. This echoes something we mentioned earlier – that we are spiritual beings having a human experience. Many people who have had a near-death experience perceive themselves simply as pure consciousness without any great awareness of, or dependence on, a physical body – and their powers of perception are greatly enhanced, rather than diminished, by being "out of the body." One of the best-known researchers of near-death experiences is Swiss-born psychiatrist Dr. Elisabeth Kubler-Ross.

Perhaps more than any other person, Dr. Kubler-Ross is associated with the process of death and dying. She is also personally convinced about the evidence for an afterlife. For her it is no longer a matter of belief, but rather a matter of knowing.

Dr. Kubler-Ross says that her views are based on a personal study of more than 20,000 people who have had near-death experiences. She has noted that many dying subjects experience a distinct separation of body and consciousness – sometimes to the extent of looking down on their bodies in a hospital or at the scene of an accident. Dr. Kubler-Ross also says quite categorically that none of her patients who has had an out-of-body experience was ever again afraid to die. In her view, death may be considered as the discarding of one's physical form and a transition to a different state of conscious awareness: "Death is simply a shedding of the physical body like the butterfly shedding its cocoon. It is a transition to a higher state of consciousness where you continue to perceive, to understand, to laugh, and to be able to grow. The only thing you lose is something that you don't need anymore, your physical body. It's like putting away your winter coat when spring comes. You know that the coat is shabby and you don't want to wear it anymore. That's virtually what death is about." Dr. Kubler-Ross believes that none of us dies alone, that those of our loved ones who have preceded us in death will be there to assist our transition through death, and that death, like life, is "a birth into a different existence." According to Dr. Kubler-Ross, the experience of passing through death is profoundly uplifting: "After we pass through this visually very beautiful and individually appropriate form of transition … we are approaching a source of light that many of our patients describe and that I myself experienced in the form of an incredibly beautiful and unforgettable life-changing experience. This is called cosmic consciousness. In the presence of this light, which most people in our western hemisphere call Christ or God, or love or light, we are surrounded by total and absolute unconditional love, understanding and compassion."

CAN WE BE REBORN?

Many people who have near-death experiences return with the realization that the physical world is like a school where one learns the essential lessons of life. As these lessons are learned, one progresses through the different levels of spiritual evolution. This in turn leads us to consider the idea that we may each have to experience many different lives on Earth, and that we have to undergo a continuing cycle of rebirths until the lessons of life are learned.

Only one breath separates
us from the next life.
If we do not reflect on death
in the morning, we will waste
the day; if we do not
reflect on death in the evening,
we will waste the night.

Karma Lekshe Tsomo

The idea that we can be reborn – that we can live more than one life on Earth – is essentially an Eastern idea and is not part of Jewish, Christian or Islamic religious teaching. Nevertheless, increasing numbers of people in the West are now rejecting religious orthodoxy and have come to believe in the possibility of reincarnation or spiritual rebirth.

One of the most important distinctions between the major Eastern and Western religions is that Eastern traditions such as Hinduism and Buddhism emphasize endless cycles of cosmic time without beginning or end, in which the Universe and all living beings experience countless transformations. Western religions such as Judaism, Christianity and Islam, on the other hand, conceive of the Creation followed by a spiritual revelation and then a Final Judgment. Expressed concisely, Eastern religions embrace infinite cycles of time, whereas Western religions deal with finite beginnings and endings. This produces a very different style of religious belief.

Followers of the orthodox Jewish, Christian or Islamic religions are likely to believe that their spiritual salvation depends very much on a personal decision to commit themselves to the God of their faith, and that the consequences of this decision – made in the present lifetime – will last for all eternity in the afterlife. Most Jews, Christians and Muslims reject the idea of reincarnation completely

After death, when most of you for the first time realize
what life here is all about, you will begin to see that
your life here is almost nothing but the sum total of
every choice you have made during every moment of
your life. Your thoughts, which you are responsible for,
are as real as your deeds. You will begin to realize that
every word and every deed affects your life and also
touches thousands of lives.

DR. ELISABETH KUBLER-ROSS

The more we accept death, the more it will be easier for us to discover a true direction in life. Accepting death frees us to love life to its fullest, and to discover a happiness and joy in being alive. If we refuse to accept death, we can only stagger blindly through our lives, with no idea of what we really want or need, or where we are going.

SOGYAL RINPOCHE

and maintain that we only have one life, given as a gift from God, in which to make the journey towards spiritual salvation.

However, in the Eastern religions it is generally accepted that an individual has many lifetimes to achieve spiritual transformation and liberation. Each new day brings fresh opportunities for spiritual lessons and insight, and each lifetime flows on from one to the next.

Most people who believe in reincarnation accept that one lifetime simply isn't enough time to absorb and integrate all the lessons that human experience presents. It therefore makes good sense to accept that a succession of lives, or incarnations, is part of the journey towards enlightenment.

According to this perspective, our individual human lives are very much part of a greater cycle of evolutionary development, and the seemingly endless cycle of individual births, deaths and rebirths makes it possible for the spiritual lessons of life to be learned and assimilated. It nevertheless remains our individual responsibility to embrace the challenges and experiences of everyday life and learn from them.

The Dalai Lama offers some fascinating insights on reincarnation in relation to how we should live our lives, especially with regard to the need for tolerance and compassion in our dealings with other people. In his view, in the same way that we naturally feel an instinctive bond with members of our own immediate family, we should also extend this feeling of connection to the broad sweep of humanity because through our numerous lifetimes on this earth – experienced through the endless cycles of rebirth – we are actually all related to each other! Our father or mother in this lifetime may have been our son or daughter in an earlier life. Our friend, neighbor or antagonist this time around may have been someone we knew in an earlier period.

According to the Dalai Lama, the really important point is that we are all one family – one collective consciousness – whether we choose to recognize it or not. This means that we have to learn to work through all of our emotional reactions in our encounters with each other – whether we perceive someone as friend or foe – until we finally realize that all our conflicts are really within ourselves.

This is certainly a powerful message for the troubled times in which we live. Even if we reject the concept of reincarnation as being outside our range of religious beliefs, we can nevertheless seek to greatly improve the nature of our interactions with other people. We can all begin to act as if we are part of one human family and one collective consciousness. In this way, whether we accept the idea of reincarnation or not, the world will certainly become a better place for all of us.

At the moment we are blessed with human life and with all the possibilities that this implies. Unlike animals and lower life forms, we are able to pluck the fruit of enlightenment, an act of ultimate goodness to both ourselves and others. However, death is pressing upon us from every side, threatening to rob us of this precious opportunity at any moment, and when we die nothing can be taken with us but the seeds of our life's work and our spiritual knowledge.

HIS HOLINESS THE DALAI LAMA

Death is simply a shedding of the physical body like the butterfly shedding its cocoon. It is a transition to a higher state of consciousness where you continue to perceive, to understand, to laugh, and to be able to grow. The only thing you lose is something that you don't need anymore, your physical body. It's like putting away your winter coat when spring comes. You know that the coat is shabby and you don't want to wear it anymore. That's virtually what death is about.

DR. ELISABETH KUBLER-ROSS

Death is a friend, not an enemy.
It brings to a close all that
can be done in this lifetime.
If there is unfinished business
one can rest assured it will be resolved,
either after death or in the next life.

Z'EV BEN SHIMON HALEVI

I don't know what your
destiny will be, but one thing I know:
the only ones among you
who will be really happy are
those who have sought and found
how to serve.

ALBERT SCHWEITZER

A WAY FORWARD

At a gathering of the Arizona Hopi Nation in August 1999, Don Evegouma, a 107-year-old Hopi elder, greeted his people with these words:

> You have been telling people that this is the eleventh hour. Now, you must go back and tell the people that this is the hour. There are things to consider …
>
> Where are you living? What are you doing?
> What are your relationships? Are you in the right relation?
> Where is your water? Know your garden.
> It is time to speak your truth. Create your community.
> Be good to each other.
> And do not look outside yourself for the leader …

He continued:

> The elders say we must let go of the shore, push off into the middle of

the river, keep our eyes open and our heads above water … At this time in our history, we should take nothing personally, least of all ourselves. For the moment that we do, our spiritual growth journey comes to a halt. The time of the lone wolf is over. Gather yourselves! All that we do now must be done in a sacred moment, and in celebration. We are the ones we have been waiting for!

We are the times, we are the people … *we* are the ones we have been waiting for. Don Evegouma's powerful words are clearly relevant not only to the Hopi people, but to us all. Now is undoubtedly the time to *act*, now is the time to *be*, now is the time to *cooperate* – with all those with whom we come into contact, and with Nature herself. We are all human beings sharing different parts of this beautiful planet. We are all members of one global family, and no life is worth more than another life. It is life itself that is a gift to celebrate. Geographical borders are nothing other than surface scars on the face of our mother Earth – they do not exist when the planet is viewed from outer space. Our superficial skin colors and cultures have an adaptive and evolutionary purpose. These have changed, and will change again and again, over time. Only the eternal treasure house within does not change. And all of us share that one Reality – if only we could seek within to know and embrace it.

Why not seek some level of awareness
where we don't create these problems for
ourselves all the time? Let's not just ask for
a new job, a new relationship, or a new
body. Let's ask for a new world; let's ask for
a new life … The return to love is not the
end of life's adventure, but the beginning.
It's the return to who you really are.

MARIANNE WILLIAMSON

The only journey is
The one within.

RAINER MARIA RILKE

It is now time to move beyond creating enemies, to look inside ourselves and courageously face our fears, conflicts and wearying negativity. It is time to welcome back those aspects of ourselves which we have found too difficult to acknowledge, too painful to bear. It is time to move beyond intolerance, and even an "attitude" of tolerance, and to celebrate the differences and diversity that is the very nature of life itself – and which gives existence its color and vitality. We have tried other ways and they have not worked in making us happier, or the world a better, more harmonious place to live. In fact, the opposite appears to be the case: the world's peoples seem to be now more miserable, more depressed, more addicted, more polarized, more deprived en masse than ever before – while a few anxiously luxuriate in increasingly deadening materialism.

How can we not realize that we have been sold a bill of non-rights that is not working for most of the people on this planet? We are poisoning the Earth, the air and the waterways, and in doing this we are poisoning ourselves and all other species – many of whom we depend on for life.

What is it that we are waiting for? No-one is going to "save us" from ourselves, and why should they? – for it is up to us to "save" ourselves. And there is no escape – retreating behind fantasy screens of one kind and another is a tacit complicity in the continuing desecration

... Can you hear the spaces between the phrases?

The silent screams getting louder? ...

Is it oppressor, oppressed, oppressor –

In ceaseless cycle, unholy war?

Or the dawn of a new age morning –

Polychromatic phoenix, harmony's door?

For events cast shadows before entering,

Leave footprints on departing.

Sssh – can you hear sleeping souls stirring

to a vision from the Dreaming?

In a sacred manner, he walks,

In a sacred manner, she talks ...

UMA AMRITANANDA

of our various environments: internal and external, physical and spiritual. Meanwhile, the global crisis deepens and the dangers increase until "suddenly" the consequences of our actions appear on our doorsteps and smash down the walls of our denial and resistance.

Whether we want to or not, whether we like it or not, it is time now for us all to wake up, and to grow out of our immature dependencies – to individually and collectively take responsibility for our lives and our earthly and spiritual homes. It is time for us to discover the joy and the love that is our true nature, and which makes life worth living. These are ways forward, and, if these seem like strong words, they are nevertheless an expression of tough, compassionate love.

Fundamentally, while on one level we all have to go it alone, we are never really alone with the Divine in our heart. We all wish for the same things for ourselves and for those in our circle of care. And, although we are inclined to care more for those whom destiny has designated family and friends, can we really afford to care less about the fate of those who are not in our immediate physical sphere? For we are all interdependent: earth, animal, plant, human, air, water, sun, moon, visible and non-visible spheres alike … we all share existence … we are all constituted of the same stuff of matter and non-matter. Strike against one aspect of life and you strike against the whole, care for one aspect of existence and you care for the whole. Each and every one of us is responsible for what we think, for what we feel, for what we do – and for what we don't do. Each in our own individual way is designed to play a part in our evolution towards cosmic consciousness. Now is the time, as never before, to "think globally and act locally."

As the Dalai Lama has wisely observed: "We human beings are witnessing our world growing smaller. The world, it seems, is becoming one community, one unit … We are also being drawn together by the very serious problems we face: over-population, dwindling natural resources, and an environmental crisis. These threaten the very foundation of existence on this one small planet we share … To meet the challenge of our times, I believe that humanity must develop a greater sense of universal responsibility. Each of us must learn to work not just for our own individual self, family, or nation, but for the benefit of all … Universal responsibility is the real key to human survival."

It is also time for us to move beyond religious and political division and to recognize that all human beings have a basic right to choose their own path to Divine Reality. This is expressed in individual ways in various cultures, but all of the major wisdom traditions – from ancient times to the present – affirm that at a deep and profound

Meditate within eternity

Don't stay in the mind

Your thoughts are like a child fretting

near its mother's breast, restless and

afraid, who with a little guidance, can

find the path of courage.

LALLA

Absorption in the heart of being,

Whence we sprang,

Is the path of action, of devotion,

Of union and of knowledge.

BHAGAVAN SRI RAMANA MAHARSHI

level of our being we are all one in Spirit. A major obstacle in these troubled times, as Larry Dossey has expressed it, is that we see division and conflict where instead we should embrace wholeness and harmony: "The Earth is together; it is we who are fragmented. If we hope to play any lasting role in what occurs on our planet, we must recover our lost unity." Now is the time when consciousness of the infinite dimension of existence needs to be cultivated in our lives. To seek it, to find it, and to live it, is a way forward.

Life will always have its ups and downs, its bright days and its dull days, its troubled times and its harmonious times – and you get on with life anyway. Many wise people say that the key is to live from the heart. Life is immeasurably happier if lived authentically, courageously, respectfully, responsibly, peaceably, gratefully, soulfully, lovingly, beautifully, compassionately.

To thine own self be true.

WILLIAM SHAKESPEARE

Imagine all the people

sharing all the world ...

JOHN LENNON

The breeze at dawn has secrets to tell you.

Don't go back to sleep.

You must ask for what you really want.

Don't go back to sleep.

… The door is round and open.

Don't go back to sleep!

RUMI

FURTHER READING

Aurobindo, Sri, *The Essential Aurobindo*, Lindisfarne Books, Herndon, Virginia 1999

Boldt, Laurence G., *How to Be, Do or Have Anything*, Ten Speed Press, Berkeley 2001

Campbell, Joseph, *Myths to Live By*, Viking, New York 1993

Chodron, Pema, *Start Where You Are*, Shambhala, Boston 1994

Chopra, Deepak, *The Deeper Wound*, Crown, New York 2001

Dalai Lama, *Ancient Wisdom, Modern World*, Little Brown, London 2001

Dalai Lama, *The Meaning of Life*, Wisdom Publications, Boston 2000

Das, Lama Surya, *Awakening the Buddha Within*, Bantam, New York 1998

Dossey, Larry, *Prayer is Good Medicine*, HarperCollins, San Francisco 1996

Dowrick, Stephanie, *Forgiveness and Other Acts of Love*, Norton, New York 1998

Gimbutas, Marija, *The Living Goddesses*, University of California Press, Berkeley 2001

Godman, David (ed.), *Be As You Are: The Teachings of Sri Ramana Maharshi*, Arkana, London 1985

Holbeche, Soozi, *Changes*, London Bridge, London 1998

Jeffers, Susan, *Face the Fear and Do it Anyway*, Fawcett, New York 1996

Jung, Carl, *Memories, Dreams, Reflections*, Pantheon, New York 1961

Khan, Hazrat Inayat, *Mastery Through Accomplishment*, Omega Publications, New Lebanon, New York 1993

Kubler-Ross, Elisabeth, *On Life After Death*, Celestial Arts, Berkeley 1991

Millman, Dan, *Everyday Enlightenment*, Warner Books, New York 1999

Moody, Raymond, *Life After Life*, Bantam, New York 1978

Morse, Melvin, *Transformed by the Light*, Random House, New York 1992

Osho, *Everyday Osho*, Fair Winds Press, Gloucester, Massachusetts 2002

Peck, M. Scott, *People of the Lie*, Simon & Schuster, New York 1997

Ring, Kenneth, *Heading Toward Omega*, Morrow, New York 1984

Rumi, *The Essential Rumi*, translations by Coleman Barks with John Moyne, HarperCollins, San Francisco 1995

Sardello, Robert, *Freeing the Soul from Fear*, Riverhead, New York 1999

Shelton, Mary Murray, *Guidance from the Darkness*, Tarcher, New York 2000

Tolle, Eckhart, *The Power of Now*, New World Library, Novato, California 1999

Vardey, Lucinda (ed.), *God in all Worlds*, Pantheon, New York 1995

Woodman, Marion, *Addiction to Perfection*, Inner City Books, Toronto 1985

Zukav, Gary, *The Seat of the Soul*, Simon & Schuster, New York 1990

Published in 2003 by Lansdowne Publishing Pty Ltd
Level 1, 18 Argyle Street, Sydney NSW 2000, Australia

First published in the United States in 2003 by
Red Wheel/Weiser LLC
York Beach, ME
With offices at:
368 Congress Street
Boston, MA 02210
www.redwheelweiser.com

Commissioned by Deborah Nixon
Text: Anna Voigt and Nevill Drury
Design: Avril Makula
Copy Editor: Sarah Shrubb
Production Manager: Sally Stokes
Project Coordinator: Kate Merrifield

ISBN 1-59003-065-6

This book is intended to give general information only. The publishers expressly disclaim
all liability to any person arising directly or indirectly from the use of, or for any errors
or omissions in, the information in this book. The adoption and application of the
information in this book is at the reader's discretion and is his or her sole responsibility.

Set in Goudy and Frutiger on QuarkXPress
Printed in Singapore by Imago